Effective Stress Management

Developing Management Skills

Other Titles in the Series

Developing Management Skills

EFFECTIVE STRESS MANAGEMENT

David A Whetten
Kim Cameron
Mike Woods

HarperCollins*Publishers*

This edition first published in 1996 by
HarperCollins College
An imprint of HarperCollins Publishers Ltd, UK
77–85 Fulham Palace Road
Hammersmith,
London W6 8JB

Mike Woods asserts the moral right to be identified as the author of the
adapted material.

British Library Cataloguing in Publication Data. A catalogue record for this
book is available from the British Library

ISBN 0-00-4990447

Typeset by Dorchester Typesetting Group Ltd
Printed and bound by Scotprint Ltd, Musselburgh
Cover design: The Senate

Contents

Preface

Effective Stress Management is one of a series of six books based on *Developing Management Skills for Europe*, a major work by David Whetton, Kim Cameron and Mike Woods. The other titles are *Effective Conflict Managment*, *Effective Communication*, *Effective Empowerment and Delegation*, *Effective Problem-Solving* and *Effective Motivation*. Presented in a convenient form this series provides a background of reading and exercises for tutors and students taking MBA grade or other business qualifications.

Each book seeks to find a balance between a sound theoretical background and relevant case studies. Our objective remains, as it did in the combined work, to develop behavioural skills not only to increase knowledge and understanding in the area but also to enable students to apply what they have learned. We hope our readers will achieve their qualifications and become productive members of their organisations by learning applicable skills.

The structure of the books and the method of teaching they employ are, in our opinion unique. Each book begins with a series of questionnaires designed to check on the reader's present understanding of the area, and in some cases assist the reader in self assessment. Thus in the present book, *Effective Stress Management*, the reader is asked to rate his or her ability to manage stress and to look at their time management skills. Further into the book, additional questionnaires look at the reader's personality type and the external issues that are likely to impinge on their resistance to work stresses. From these questionnaires the reader will be able to set learning objectives for the book, and on finishing the text, see how much he or she has been able to relate to the very personal world of self.

The main body of the text provides a theoretical background to the issues of personal stress and firm pointers to personal strategies so that the reader can survive and prosper in the inevitable stress-soaked environment of the real world. The text closes with two case studies, discussion questions, exercises and a section on Application Planning.

Our firm belief is that when 'all is said and done, there is more said than done'. We are asking our readers to make a real commitment to use the material and become more effective in their chosen professions.

Introduction

Stress, like change is an ever present and growing element in our lives, as students and as managers. Unfortunately many books on stress tend to deal with the clinical aspects – they are not designed for 'well people'. In this book we hope to strike a balance. We accept that stress is a part of all our working lives and that without stress not only would things be intolerable dull, for most of us, but also very few things would be done. Tolerable levels of stress are the winding mechanism of our world. As individuals we develop strategies to deal with accustomed levels of stress. We have simple techniques for dealing with temporary surges and stronger techniques for negotiating our way out of uncomfortable but predictable pressures. We can 'stand on the shoulders' of those before us and learn from their skills and application. However, we also need to recognise that prolonged and personally intolerable levels of stress can lead to serious illness; although we have, as right, the alternative of engineering our lives so that this does not occur.

This book does not suggest that we all take up croft farming in one of the remote places of the world, but that there are easily acquired skills that will make our lives longer, more personally fulfilling and fruitful, without a total change in our standard of living. These skills will assist us in our study and make us more efficient and effective in our jobs. By learning about stress in what we feel is a stress-free way, we will not only help ourselves but those around us – stress is a contagious disease. Therefore, we are offering a diagnosis, a prognosis and helpful advice towards a cure, all of which you can practice in the safety of these pages before trying them out in what you may find to be an unforgiving world.

Skill Pre-assessment

Diagnostic Surveys for Managing Stress

Introduction

The following questionnaires are designed to:

■ Explore you own responses to situations you may find stressful.

■ Look at the techniques you use to manage your own time.

■ Help you establish a personality *type*.

■ Consider the outside factors that may cause you to yield to situations where one would normally expect to cope.

Please complete the questionnaires before reading the book and in the case of the first questionnaire, return to it after reading the book to see how the material has related to your personal world, thus allowing you to set your own Application Plans accordingly.

Stress Management

Instructions

Step 1: For each statement write a number on the rating scale in the Pre-assessment column on the left. Your answers should reflect your attitudes and behaviour as they are now, not as you would like them to be. Be honest. When you have completed the survey, use the Scoring Key at the end of the book (page 92), to identify the skill areas discussed that are most important for you to master. Improving these skill areas should provide you with your learning objectives.

Step 2: When you have completed the book and the Skill Application assignments, review your responses in the right hand Post-assessment column. When you have completed the survey, use the Scoring Key at the end of the book (page 92) to measure your progress. If your score remains low in specific skill areas, use the behavioural guidelines at the end of the Skill Learning section (page 70) to guide your Application Planning.

Rating Scale

6 = Strongly agree   5 = Agree   4 = Slightly agree
3 = Slightly disagree   2 = Disagree   1 = Strongly disagree

ASSESSMENT

PRE-   POST-   **When faced with stressful or time-pressured situations –**

_____ _____ 1. I use a variety of techniques – making lists, setting priorities, time diaries – to manage my time effectively.

_____ _____ 2. I maintain a programme of regular exercise for fitness.

_____ _____ 3. I maintain an open, trusting relationship with someone with whom I can share my frustrations.

_____ _____ 4. I know and practice several temporary relaxation techniques such as deep breathing and muscle relaxation.

_____ _____ 5. I keep reviewing my priorities so that less important things don't drive out more important things.

_____ _____ 6. I maintain balance in my life by pursuing a variety of interests outside of work.

_____ _____ 7. I have a close relationship with someone who serves as my mentor or advisor.

_____ _____ 8. I use other people appropriately to complete what has to be done.

_____ _____ 9. I encourage others to consider solutions, not just questions, when they come to me with problems or concerns.

_____ _____ 10. I strive to redefine problems as opportunities for improvement.

When I get others to do things for me –

_____ _____ 11. I make certain that they have the necessary means and authority to do what needs to be done.

_____ _____ 12. I specify clearly what I want achieved and how much they can do without referring it back to me.

_____ _____ 13 I pass along new information and resources to those to whom I have delegated tasks.

_____ _____ 14 I make sure that the other person completely understands the results I expect when I delegate tasks.

_____ _____ 15. I follow up and maintain accountability for delegated tasks on a regular basis.

Time Management

In responding to the statements below, circle the number that indicates the frequency with which you do each activity. Assess your behaviour as it is, not as you would like it to be. How useful this questionnaire will be depends on your ability to assess your own behaviour.

The first section of the questionnaire is universal but second section is designed for working managers. Turn to end of the book to find the Scoring Key and an interpretation of your scores (page 92).

0 = Never   1 = Seldom   2 = Sometimes
3 = Usually   4 = Always

SECTION I

1. I read selectively, skimming the material until I find what is important, then highlighting it.   0 1 2 3 4
2. I make a list of tasks to accomplish each day.   0 1 2 3 4
3. I keep everything in its proper place at work.   0 1 2 3 4
4. I prioritise the tasks I have to do according to their importance and urgency.   0 1 2 3 4
5. I concentrate on only one important task at a time, but I do multiple trivial tasks at once (like signing letters while talking on the phone).   0 1 2 3 4
6. I make a list of short five- or ten-minute tasks to do.   0 1 2 3 4
7. I divide large projects into smaller, separate stages.   0 1 2 3 4
8. I identify which 20 per cent of my tasks will produce 80 per cent of the results.   0 1 2 3 4
9. I do the most important tasks at my best time during the day.   0 1 2 3 4
10. I have some time during each day when I can work uninterrupted.   0 1 2 3 4
11. I don't procrastinate. I do today what needs to be done.   0 1 2 3 4
12. I keep track of the use of my time with devices such as a time log.   0 1 2 3 4
13. I set deadlines for myself.   0 1 2 3 4
14. I do something productive whenever I am waiting.   0 1 2 3 4
15. I do redundant 'busy work' at one set time during the day.   0 1 2 3 4
16. I finish at least one thing every day.   0 1 2 3 4
17. I schedule some time during the day for personal time alone (for thinking, planning, exercise).   0 1 2 3 4

18. I allow myself to worry about things at one particular time during the day, not all the time.   0 1 2 3 4
19. I have clearly defined long-term objectives toward which I am working.   0 1 2 3 4
20. I always try to find little ways to use my time more efficiently.   0 1 2 3 4

SECTION II – for working managers only
1. I hold routine meetings at the end of the day.   0 1 2 3 4
2. I hold all short meetings standing up.   0 1 2 3 4
3. I set a time limit at the outset of each meeting.   0 1 2 3 4
4. I cancel scheduled meetings that are not necessary.   0 1 2 3 4
5. I have a written agenda for every meeting.   0 1 2 3 4
6. I stick to the agenda and reach closure on each item.   0 1 2 3 4
7. I ensure that someone takes minutes and watches the time in every meeting.   0 1 2 3 4
8. I start all meetings on time.   0 1 2 3 4
9. I have minutes of meetings prepared promptly and see that follow-up occurs promptly.   0 1 2 3 4
10. When subordinates come to me with problems, I ask them to suggest solutions.   0 1 2 3 4
11. I meet visitors in the doorway.   0 1 2 3 4
12. I go to subordinates' offices when feasible so that I can control when I leave.   0 1 2 3 4
13. I leave at least one-fourth of my day free from meetings and appointments.   0 1 2 3 4
14. I have someone else who can answer my calls and greet visitors at least some of the time.   0 1 2 3 4
15. I have one place where I can work uninterrupted.   0 1 2 3 4
16. I do something definite with every piece of paper I handle.   0 1 2 3 4
17. I keep my workplace clear of all materials except those I am working on.   0 1 2 3 4
18. I delegate tasks.   0 1 2 3 4
19. I specify the amount of personal initiative I want others to take when I assign them a task.   0 1 2 3 4
20. I am willing to let others take the credit for tasks they accomplish.   0 1 2 3 4

Type A Personality Inventory

Rate the extent to which each of the following statements is typical of you most of the time. Focus on your general way of behaving and feeling. There are no right or wrong answers. When you have finished, turn to the Scoring Key at the end of the book (page 93) to find an interpretation of your scores.

Rating Scale

3 – The statement is very typical of me.
2 – The statement is somewhat typical of me.
1 – The statement is not at all typical of me.

— 1. My greatest satisfaction comes from doing things better than others.
— 2. I tend to bring the theme of a conversation around to things I'm interested in.
— 3. In conversations, I frequently clench my fist, bang on the table or pound one fist into the palm of another for emphasis.
— 4. I move, walk and eat rapidly.
— 5. I feel as though I can accomplish more than others.
— 6. I feel guilty when I relax or do nothing for several hours or days.
— 7. It doesn't take much to get me to argue.
— 8. I feel impatient with the rate at which most events take place.
— 9. Having more than others is important to me.
— 10. One aspect of my life (e.g., work, family care, school) dominates all others.
— 11. I frequently regret not being able to control my temper.
— 12. I hurry the speech of others by saying 'Uh huh,' 'Yes, yes,' or by finishing their sentences for them.
— 13. People who avoid competition have low self-confidence.
— 14. To do something well you have to concentrate and screen out all distractions.
— 15. I feel others' mistakes and errors cause me needless aggravation.
— 16. I find it intolerable to watch others perform tasks I know I can do faster.
— 17. Getting ahead in my job is a major personal goal.
— 18. I simply don't have enough time to lead a well-balanced life.
— 19. I take out my frustration with my own imperfections on others.
— 20. I frequently try to do two or more things simultaneously.
— 21. When I encounter a competitive person, I feel a need to challenge him or her.
— 22. I tend to fill up my spare time with thoughts and activities related to my work (or family or studies).
— 23. I am frequently upset by the unfairness of life.
— 24. I find it anguishing to wait in line.

Adapted from Friedman, M., & Rosenman, R.H. Type A behaviour and your heart. New York: Knopf, 1974

Social Readjustment Rating Scale (SRRS)

Circle any of the following you have experienced in the past year. Using the weightings at the right, total up your score.

LIFE EVENT	MEAN VALUE
1. Death of spouse	100
2. Divorce	73
3. Marital separation from mate	65
4. Detention in jail or other institution	63
5. Death of a close family member	63
6. Major personal injury or illness	53
7. Marriage	50
8. Losing your job	47
9. Marital reconciliation with partner	45
10. Retirement from work	45
11. Major change in the health or behaviour of a family member	44
12. Pregnancy	40
13. Sexual difficulties	39
14. Gaining a new family member (e.g., through birth, adoption, elderly relative moving in, etc.)	39
15. Major business readjustment (e.g., merger, reorganisation, bankruptcy, etc.)	39
16. Major change in financial state (e.g., a lot worse off or a lot better off than usual)	38
17. Death of a close friend	37
18. Change to/of job	36
19. Major change in the number of arguments with spouse (e.g., either a lot more or a lot less than usual regarding childbearing, personal habits, etc.)	35
20. Taking out a mortgage or loan for a major purchase (e.g., for a home, business, etc.)	31
21. Foreclosure on a mortgage or loan	30
22. Major change in responsibilities at work (e.g., promotion, demotion, lateral transfer)	29
23. Son or daughter leaving home (e.g., marriage, attending college, etc.)	29
24. Trouble with in-laws	29
25. Outstanding personal achievement	28
26. Spouse beginning or ceasing work outside the home	26
27. Beginning or ending formal education	26
28. Major change in living conditions (e.g., new house, redecoration, deterioration of neighbourhood, etc)	25

29. Revision of personal habits (dress, manners, association, etc.) — 24
30. Troubles with the boss — 23
31. Major change in working hours or conditions — 20
32. Moving home — 20
33. Change to a new college, school, university. — 20
34. Major change in usual type and/or amount of recreation — 19
35. Major change in outside activities (e.g., a lot more/less than usual) — 19
36. Major change in social activities (e.g., clubs, dancing, cinema, visiting, etc.) — 18
37. Taking out a mortgage or loan for a lesser purchase (e.g., for a car, TV, freezer, etc.) — 17
38. Major change in sleeping habits (a lot more/less/or change in part of day when asleep, shifts) — 16
39. Major change in number of family get-togethers (e.g., a lot more/less than usual) — 15
40. Major change in eating habits (a lot more/less food, very different meal times or surroundings) — 15
41. Holiday — 13
42. Christmas — 12
43. Minor violations of the law (e.g., parking tickets, disturbing the peace) — 11

TOTAL OF CIRCLED ITEMS:

NOTE: A discussion of the SRRS scores and their significance follows in the next section, Skill Learning (see pages 22–23)

Source: T. H. Holmes and R. H. Rahe, Social Readjustment Rating Scale, Journal of Psychosomatic Research, 1967, 11, 213-218.

Sources of Personal Stress

1. Identify the factors that produce the most stress for you right now. What is it that creates feelings of stress in your life?
2. Now give each of those stressors a rating from 1 to 100 on the basis of how powerful each is in producing stress. Refer to the Social Readjustment Rating Scale for relative weightings of stressors. A rating of 100, for example, might be associated with the death of a spouse or child, while a rating of 10 might be associated with the overly slow driver in front of you.
3. Use these specific sources of stress as targets as you discuss and practice the stress management principles presented in the rest of this book.

Skill Learning

Improving the Management of Stress and Time

The problems currently associated with stress at work appear to be particularly acute in Britain, for example the British Heart Foundation has estimated that coronary heart disease costs £200 per employee per year. While some coronary heart disease may be directly attributable to stress, Davidson and Sutherland (1992) suggest that many behavioural responses to stress, such as cigarette smoking, poor dietary habits, physical inactivity and/or escapist drinking, are all risk factors for cardiovascular disease. Thus as a consequence, stress may be both directly and indirectly implicated as a causal factor in the aetiology of heart disease.

The costs of work related stress, however, extend beyond coronary heart disease. Kearns (1986) comments that 60 per cent of absence from work is caused by stress related illness, while Gill (1987) reports that approximately 100 million working days are lost each year because people cannot face going to work. Additionally Cooper *et al* (1988), note that there is mounting evidence to suggest that days lost in British Industry due to mental and stress-related causes are on the increase. This view is further endorsed by a recent estimate completed by Summers (1990) for the Confederation of British Industry, which showed the annual cost of stress-related absenteeism in labour turnover to be around £1.5 billion.

As an illustration of the debilitating effects of job-related stress, consider the following story reported by the Associated Press.

> The job was getting to the ambulance attendant. He felt disturbed by the recurring tragedy, isolated by the long shifts. His marriage was in trouble. He was drinking too much.
>
> One night it all blew up.
>
> He rode in the back that night. His partner drove. Their first call was for a man whose leg had been cut off by a train. His screaming and

agony were horrifying, but the second call was worse. It was a child beating. As the attendant treated the youngster's bruised body and snapped bones, he thought of his own child. His fury grew.

Immediately after leaving the child at the hospital, the attendants were sent out to help a heart attack victim seen lying in a street. When they arrived, however, they found not a cardiac patient but a drunk who had passed out. As they lifted the man into the ambulance, their frustration and anger came to a head. They decided to give the drunk a ride he would remember.

The ambulance vaulted over railroad tracks at high speed. The driver took the corners as fast as he could, flinging the drunk from side to side in the back. To the attendants, it was a joke.

Suddenly, the drunk began having a real heart attack. The attendant in the back leaned over the drunk and started shouting. 'Die, you fool!' he yelled. 'Die!'

He watched as the drunk shuddered. He watched as the drunk died. By the time they reached the hospital, they had their stories straight. Dead on arrival, they said. Nothing they could do.

The attendant, who must remain anonymous, talked about that night at a recent counselling session on 'professional burnout' – a growing problem in high-stress jobs.

As this story graphically illustrates, stress can produce devastating effects. Personal consequences can range from inability to concentrate, anxiety and depression to stomach disorders, low resistance to illness and heart disease. For organisations, consequences range from absenteeism and job dissatisfaction, to high accident and turnover rates.

The Role of Management

What is amazing is that a 25-year study of employee surveys revealed that incompetent management is the largest cause of workplace stress! Three out of four surveys listed employee relationships with immediate supervisors as the worst aspect of the job. Moreover, research in psychology has found that stress not only affects workers negatively, but also produces less visible (though equally detrimental) consequences for managers themselves. For example, when managers experience stress they tend to:

- Perceive information selectively and see only that which confirms their previous biases
- Become very intolerant of ambiguity and demanding of right answers
- Only consider a single approach to a problem
- Overestimate how fast time is passing (hence, they always feel rushed)
- Adopt a short-term perspective or crisis mentality and cease to consider long-term implications
- Have less ability to make fine distinctions in problems, so that complexity and nuances are missed
- Consult and listen to others less
- Rely on old habits to cope with current situations
- Have less ability to generate creative thoughts and unique solutions to problems

(Source: Staw, Sandelands, and Dutton, 1981; Weick, 1984).

In other words, not only do the results of stress affect employees in a negative way but they also reduce the effective behaviour of managers – e.g., listening, making good decisions, solving problems effectively, planning, and generating new ideas. Developing the skill of managing stress therefore, can have significant advantages to all concerned. The ability to deal appropriately with stress not only enhances individual self-development, but can also have an enormous financial impact on entire organisations.

Unfortunately, most of the scientific literature on stress focuses on its consequences. Too little examines how to cope effectively with stress and even less addresses how to prevent stress. We begin our discussion by presenting a framework for understanding stress and learning how to cope with it. Here we will explain the major types of stressors faced by managers, the primary reactions to stress and the reasons some people experience more negative reactions than others. In the last section, we will present principles for managing and adapting to stress, along with specific examples and behavioural guidelines.

Major Elements of Stress

One way to understand the dynamics of stress is to think of it as the product of a 'force field' (Lewin, 1951). Kurt Lewin suggested that all individuals and organisations exist in an environment filled with reinforcing or opposing forces (i.e., stresses). These forces act to stimulate or inhibit the performance desired by the individual. As illustrated in Figure 1, a person's level of performance in an organisation results from factors that may either complement or contradict one another. Certain forces drive or motivate changes in behaviour, while other forces restrain or block those changes.

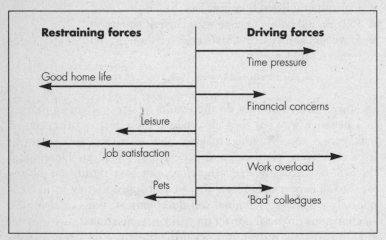

FIGURE 1   Lewin's force field – forces for stress

According to Lewin's theory, the forces affecting individuals are normally balanced in the force field. The strength of the driving forces is exactly matched by the strength of the restraining forces. (In the figure, longer arrows indicate stronger forces.) Performance changes when the forces become out of balance. That is, if the driving forces become stronger than the restraining forces, or more numerous or enduring, then change occurs. Conversely, if restraining forces become stronger or more numerous than driving forces, change occurs in the opposite direction.

Feelings of stress are a product of a combination of stressors which may come from inside the individual or from his or her environment. These stressors are the driving forces in our model; they exert pressure on the individual to change their existing levels of performance – physiologically, psychologically and interpersonally. Unrestrained, those forces can lead to pathological results (e.g., anxiety, heart disease and mental breakdown). However, most people have developed certain resiliences or restraining forces to counteract the stressors thus inhibiting their pathological effects. These restraining forces include behaviour patterns, psychological characteristics and supportive social relationships. Strong restraining forces lead to low heart rates, good interpersonal relationships, emotional stability and effective stress management. Without the restraining forces, which have to be developed by individuals over time, the stressors reign.

Of course, stress produces positive as well as negative effects. In the absence of any stress, people feel completely bored and lack any inclination to act. Even when high levels of stress are experienced, equilibrium can be restored quickly if sufficient resiliency is present. In the case of the ambulance driver, for example, multiple stressors overpowered the available restraining forces and burnout occurred. Before such an extreme state is reached, however, individuals typically progress through three stages of reactions: an alarm stage, a resistance stage, an exhaustion stage.

Reactions to Stress

The alarm stage is characterised by acute increases in anxiety or fear if the stressor is perceived as a threat, or by increases in sorrow or depression if the stressor is perceived as a loss. A feeling of shock or confusion may result if the stressor is particularly acute. Physiologically, the individual's energy resources are mobilised and heart rate, blood pressure and alertness increase. These reactions are largely self-correcting if the stressor is of brief duration. However, if it continues, the individual enters the resistance stage, in which defence mechanisms predominate and the body begins to store up excess energy.

Five types of defence mechanisms are typical of most people who experience extended levels of stress. The first is aggression, which involves attacking the stressor directly. It may also involve attacking oneself, other people or even objects (e.g., kicking the table). A second is regression, which is the adoption of a behaviour pattern or response that was successful at some earlier time (e.g., responding in childish ways). A third defence mechanism, repression, involves denial of the stressor, forgetting or redefining the stressor (e.g., deciding that it isn't so scary after all). Withdrawal is a fourth defence mechanism, which may take both psychological and physical forms. Individuals may engage in fantasy, inattention or purposive forgetting, or they may actually escape from the situation itself. Finally, there is fixation, where a response is repeated regardless of its effectiveness (e.g., repeatedly re-dialling a telephone number).

If these defence mechanisms reduce a person's feeling of stress, negative effects such as high blood pressure, anxiety or mental disorders can be avoided and the only signs of prolonged stress may be an increase in apparent defensiveness. However, when stress is so pronounced as to overwhelm defences or so enduring as to outlast available energy for defensiveness, exhaustion may result, producing pathological consequences.

While each reaction stage may be experienced as temporarily uncomfortable, the exhaustion stage is the most dangerous one. When stressors overpower or outlast the resiliency capacities of individuals, or their ability to defend against them, chronic stress is experienced and negative personal and organisational consequences generally follow. Such pathological consequences may manifest themselves physiologically (e.g., heart disease), psychologically, (e.g., severe depression) or interpersonally (e.g., dissolution of relationships). They result from the damage done to an individual for which there was no defence (e.g., psychotic reactions among prisoners of war), from an inability to defend continuously against a stressor (e.g., becoming exhausted), from an over-reaction (e.g., an ulcer produced by excessive secretion of body chemicals) or from lack of self-awareness so that stress is completely unacknowledged.

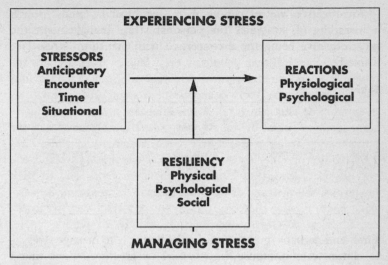

FIGURE 2 A general model of stress

Figure 2 identifies the major categories of stressors (driving forces) that managers experience, as well as the major attributes of resilience (restraining forces) that inhibit the negative aspects of stress.

Coping with Stress

Individuals vary in the extent to which they are affected by stress. Some people are what Eliot and Breo (1984) labelled 'hot reactors', meaning they have a predisposition to experience extremely negative reactions to stress. For others, stress has less serious consequences. Some athletes do better in 'the big game', while others do worse. Some managers appear to be brilliant strategists when the stakes are high; others fold under the pressure.

Our physical condition, personality characteristics and social support mechanisms work with us producing resiliency or the capacity to cope effectively with stress. In effect, resiliency serves as a form of inoculation against the effects of stress. It eliminates exhaustion.

An effective way of coping with stress can be seen through a hierarchy of strategies for personal stress management, the most effective being those concerned with managing stress (see Table 1).

Table 1

	Eliminate stressors	Develop strategies for resilience	Learn temporary coping mechanisms
Effects	Permanent	Long term	Short term
Approach	Enactive – revise the environment	Proactive	Reactive
Time scale	Long term	Medium term	Immediate

First, and perhaps most obviously, the best way to manage stress is to eliminate or minimise the stressors by creating or enacting a new environment for the individual – the *enactive strategy* (Weick, 1979). However, this is often more easily said than done and we have to resort to the second approach: increasing the overall capacity to handle stress by developing personal resiliency – the *proactive strategy*. Both these strategies take time thus pragmatic short-term techniques may be adopted where an immediate response is required – the *reactive strategy*. Reactive strategies can be applied on-the-spot as temporary remedies against the ill effects of stress.

To understand why the above hierarchy of stress management techniques is recommended, consider the following analogy. When the human body experiences a stressor, it reacts like a car engine when the driver steps on the accelerator pedal – it 'revs up'. The body releases chemicals, such as adrenaline and cortisone, that increase the heart and breathing rates, blood flow, energy level and so on. A continual or repetitive revving up of the body's engine can have the same damaging or toxic consequences over time as racing a car's engine without driving it anywhere. Burnout occurs.

Individuals are better off if they can eliminate harmful stressors and the potentially negative effects of frequent, potent stress reactions. However, because most individuals do not have complete control over their environment or their circumstances, they can seldom eliminate all harmful stressors. Their next best alternative therefore, is to develop a greater capacity to withstand the negative effects of stress and to mobilise the energy generated by stressors. Developing personal resiliency that helps the body return to normal levels of activity more quickly – or that directs the 'revved up engine' in a productive direction – is the next best strategy to eliminating the stressors altogether. Finally, on a temporary basis, individuals can respond to the revved up state by using constructive strategies such as temporary relaxation techniques and mind control. Such techniques are designed to help the 'engine' return to idle more quickly, at least for a short period of time.

Unfortunately, most people reverse the order of coping strategies presented above – i.e., they rely first on temporary reactive methods to cope with stress because these actions can be implemented immediately. But reactive strategies also have to be repeated whenever stressors are encountered because their effects are short-lived. Moreover, some common reactive strategies, such as drinking, taking sleeping pills or letting off steam through anger, can become habit-forming and harmful in themselves. Without more long-term strategies, relying on repetitive reactive strategies can create a vicious circle.

It takes more effort to develop proactive resiliency strategies, but the effects are more long-lasting. However, resiliency strategies can take time to implement; hence, the payoff, while substantial, is not immediate. The best and most permanent strategies are those that eliminate stressors altogether. They require the longest time to implement and may involve complex arrangements. But because the stress is purged, the payoff is enduring.

Managing Stress

In the following sections, each of the three components of the stress model (Figure 2) is discussed in detail. In each section we first describe the elements of the model and then discuss specific techniques for effectively managing that aspect of stress. Because elimination of stress is the most important stress management tool, we will discuss it in greater detail.

Stressors

Referring back to the case study of the ambulance driver we find four classifications of stressors, demonstrated in Table 2.

Table 2 Sources of stress

TIME STRESSORS	SITUATIONAL STRESSORS
■ Work overload	■ Unfavourable working conditions
■ Lack of control	■ Rapid change
ENCOUNTER STRESSORS	**ANTICIPATORY STRESSORS**
■ Role conflicts	■ Unpleasant expectations
■ Issue conflicts	■ Fear
■ Action conflicts	

The first, *time stressors*, generally result from having too much to do in too little time. These are the most common and most pervasive sources of stress faced by managers in corporations (Mintzberg, 1973; Carlson, 1951; Sayles, 1964).

Our culture is extremely time conscious and continues to be even more so year by year; this fascination with time makes it an important source of stress. A variety of researchers, for example, have studied the relationships between being expected to take on an increasing range of potentially conflicting, ambiguous responsibilities and chronic time pressures, against the psychological and physiological dysfunctions (French and Caplan, 1972). The researchers found significant relationships between the presence of time stressors and job dissatisfaction, tension, perceived threat, heart rate, cholesterol levels, skin resistance and other factors.

In the story of the ambulance drivers presented earlier, time stressors were evidenced by the drivers' work overload – that is, they felt compelled to accomplish a large number of tasks in a short time, but were not in control of the time available. When experienced on a daily basis, time stressors can be highly detrimental. The presence of temporary time stressors however may serve as motivators for getting work done; some individuals accomplish much more when faced with an immediate deadline than when left to work at their own pace. Against this, a constant state of time pressure – having too much to do and not enough time to do it – is usually harmful.

Encounter stressors are those that result from flawed interpersonal interactions. Most people have experienced the debilitating effects of a quarrel with a friend, flatmate, or spouse; of trying to work with an employee or supervisor with whom there has been an interpersonal conflict; or trying to accomplish a task in a group that is divided by lack of trust and cohesion. Encounter stressors result from some kind of interpersonal encounter involving conflict and are especially common for managers. They generally arise from three types of conflicts: role conflicts, in which roles performed by group members are incompatible; issue conflicts, in which disagreement exists over how to define or solve a problem; and interaction conflicts, in which individuals fail to get along well because of mutual antagonism (Hamner and Organ, 1978).

Poor relationships with others cause particularly high levels of stress. In our own research we have found that encounter stressors in organisations can reduce both work satisfaction and actual productivity (Cameron, 1994; Cameron and Whetten, 1987). Other workers have found encounter stressors to be at the very heart of most organisational dysfunction (Likert, 1967), most frequently affecting managers with responsibility for people rather than equipment. The highest levels of encounter stress exist among managers who interact frequently with other people and have responsibility for individuals in the workplace (French and Caplan, 1972). Mishra (1993), reviewer of literature on interpersonal trust, showed that a lack of trust among individuals not only blocks effective communication, information sharing, decision competence and problem-solving capabilities, but also results in high levels of personal stress. In a United States survey of workers, 'encounter stressors' were cited as a major cause of burnout. When workers were reported as feeling not free to interact socially, experiencing workplace conflict, not being able to talk openly to managers; feeling unsupported by fellow employees, being stifled by red tape and not feeling recognised, burnout was significantly higher than when those encounter stressors were not present. Of the ten most significant stressors associated with burnout, seven dealt with encounter stressors. The other three were situational stressors, to which we turn next.

Situational stressors arise from the environment in which a person lives or from an individual's circumstances. One of the most common forms of situational stress is a poor working environment. For the ambulance drivers, for example, this would include continual crises, long hours and isolation from colleagues.

One of the most well-researched links between situational stressors and negative consequences involves rapid change, particularly the effects of changes in life events (Wolff *et al.*, 1950; Holmes and Rahe, 1970). The Social Readjustment Rating Scale (SRRS) was introduced in 1967 to track the number of changes individuals had experienced over the past twelve months. Since changes in some events were thought to be more stressful than others, a scaling method was used to assign weights to each life event. Numerous studies among a variety of cultures, age groups and occupations have confirmed the relative weightings in the 1967 instrument (see Rahe *et al.*, 1980) which generally hold true regardless of culture, age or occupation. You completed this instrument in the Pre-assessment section and may like to look at your own rating now.

Statistical relationships between the amount of life-event change and physical illness and injury have been found consistently among managers (Kobasa, 1979), sports figures (Holmes and Masuda, 1974), naval personnel (Rahe, 1974), and the general population (Jenkins, 1976). For example, scores of 150 points or below result in a probability of less than 37 per cent that a serious illness will occur in the next year, but the probability increases to about 50 per cent with scores of 150–300. Those who score over 300 on the SRRS have an 80 per cent chance of serious illness (Holmes and Rahe, 1967).

Holmes and Holmes (1970) studied the extent to which daily health changes occurred as a result of life-event changes. Rather than focusing on major illness or injuries, they recorded minor symptoms such as headache, nausea, fever, backache, eyestrain, etc., over 1,300 workdays. The results revealed high correlation's between scores in life-event changes and the chronic presence of these symptoms.

We must caution, of course, that scoring high on the SRRS does not necessarily mean a person is going to become ill or be injured. A variety of coping skills and personal characteristics, to be discussed later, may counteract those tendencies. The point to be made here is that situational stressors are important factors to consider in learning to manage stress skilfully. For example, we were using the SRRS with a group of Hungarian managers, one of whom was an interpreter. She reported that in one year of her life she had a score of over 300. Wanting to talk she explained that she had been release from Auswitz, got married and had her first child – all in one year. In 1995 she still looked remarkably well.

Anticipatory stressors, the fourth category, includes potentially disagreeable events that threaten to occur – unpleasant things that have not yet happened, but might happen. Stress results from the anticipation or fear of the event. In the case of the ambulance drivers, the constant threat of anticipating having to witness one more incident of human suffering or death served as an anticipatory stressor. Western hostages in Iran and Beirut, for example, were heavily stressed by threats of death or punishment by their kidnapper guards. Schein (1960) reported that dramatic behavioural and psychological changes occurred in American prisoners in the Korean War. He identified anticipatory stressors (e.g., threat of severe punishment) as major contributors to psychological and physiological pathology among the prisoners.

Anticipatory stressors need not be highly unpleasant or severe, however, to produce stress. For example, Schachter (1959), Milgram (1963) and others induced high levels of stress by telling individuals that they would experience a loud noise or a mild shock, or that someone else might become uncomfortable because of their actions. Fear of failure or fear of embarrassment in front of peers is a common anticipatory stressor. Anxieties about retirement and losing vitality during middle age have been identified by Levinson (1978), Hall (1976) and others as common stress producers as well.

Eliminating Stressors

Because eliminating stressors is a permanent stress reduction strategy, it is by far the most desirable. It would be impossible, and perhaps not even an advantage, for individuals to eliminate all the stressors they encounter, but they can effectively eliminate those that are harmful. One way is to 'enact' the environment rather than merely 'reacting' to it (Weick, 1979). That is, individuals can actively work to create more favourable environmental circumstances in which to work and live. By so doing, they can rationally and systematically eliminate stressors. Table 3 outlines several ways in which the four kinds of stressors can be eliminated.

Table 3 Management strategies for the elimination of stress

Type of stressor	Elimination strategy
Time	Time Management
	Delegation
Encounter	Collaboration
	Interpersonal competence
Situational	Work redesign
Anticipatory	Setting priorities
	Planning

Eliminating Time Stressors Through Time Management

We have already stated that time stressors often are the greatest sources of stress for managers. Research by Mintzberg (1973) and Kotter (1987) showed, for example, that managers experience frequent interruptions (over 50 per cent of their activities last nine minutes or less); they seldom engage in long-range planning but allow fragmentation, brevity and variety to characterise their time use. On the average, no manager works more than twenty minutes at a time without interruption, and most of a manager's time is controlled by the most tiresome, persistent and energetic people (Carlson, 1951). Guest (1956) found that an industrial foreman engages in between 237 and 1,073 separate incidents a day with no real breaks. Effective time management can enable managers to gain control over their time and to organise their fragmented, chaotic environment.

Two different sets of skills are important for managing time effectively and for eliminating time stressors. The first focuses on efficiently using time on a daily basis while the second focuses on effectively using time over the long-term. Because the effectiveness approach to time management serves as the foundation for the efficiency approach, we will explain it first. We will then review the tools and techniques for achieving efficiency in time use.

Effective Time Management

Overload and lack of control are the greatest source of time stress for most of us – managers or not. Somehow, no matter how much time is available, it seems to get filled up and squeezed out. Probably the most commonly prescribed solutions for attacking problems of time stress are to use diaries and planners, to generate 'to-do' lists, and to learn to say 'no'. But although almost everyone has tried such tactics, nearly all still claim to be under enormous time stress. This is not to say that calendars, lists and saying 'no' are never useful, however they are examples of an efficiency approach to time management rather than an effectiveness approach. In eliminating time stressors, efficiency without effectiveness is fruitless.

Managing time with an effectiveness approach means that:

- Individuals spend their time on important matters, not just urgent matters
- People are able to distinguish clearly between what they view as important versus what they view as urgent
- Results rather than methods are the focus of time management strategies

■ People have a reason not to feel guilty when they must say 'no'

A number of time management experts have pointed out the usefulness of a 'time management matrix' in which activities are categorised in terms of their relative importance and urgency (Covey, 1988). Important activities are those that produce a desired result – they accomplish a valued end or they achieve a meaningful purpose. Urgent activities are those that demand immediate attention. They are associated with a need expressed by someone else, or they relate to an uncomfortable problem or situation that requires a solution as soon as possible. Figure 3 outlines this matrix and provides examples of types of activities that fit in each quadrant.

Cell 1 Important/ Urgent	**Cell 2 Unimportant/Urgent**
Examples:	Examples:
Crisis	Mail
Customer Complaints	Ringing telephones
	Unscheduled interruptions
Cell 3 Important/Non-Urgent	**Cell 4 Unimportant/Non-Urgent**
Examples:	Examples:
Developments – innovations	Routines and rituals
Planning	Arguments

FIGURE 3   The time management matrix

Activities such as handling employee crises or customer complaints are both *urgent* and *important*. A ringing telephone, the arrival of the post or unscheduled interruptions might be examples of *urgent but potentially unimportant* activities. *Important but non-urgent* activities include developmental opportunities, innovating, planning and so on.

Unimportant and *non-urgent* activities are escapes and routines that people may pursue but which produce little valuable payoff – for example, small talk, daydreaming, shuffling paper and arguing.

Activities in the *Important/Urgent* quadrant (Cell 1) usually dominate the lives of managers. They are seen as 'have to' activities that demand immediate attention. Attending a meeting, responding to a call or request, interacting with a customer, or completing a report might all legitimately be defined as important/urgent activities. The trouble with spending all one's time on activities in this quadrant, however, is that they all require the manager to react. They are usually controlled by someone else, and they may or may not lead to a result the manager wants to achieve.

The problem is even worse in the *Unimportant/Urgent* quadrant (Cell 2). Demands by others that may meet their needs but that serve only as deflections or interruptions to the manager's agenda only escalate a sense of time stress. Because we may not achieve results that are meaningful, purposeful and valued – i.e., important – feelings of time stress will never be overcome. Experiencing overload and loss of control can be guaranteed. All of us, managers included, are simply reactive.

Moreover, when these time stressors are experienced over an extended period of time, people generally try to escape into *Non-important/Non-urgent activities* (Cell 4) to relieve the stress. They escape, shut out the world or put everything on hold. But although feelings of stress may be temporarily relieved, no long-term solutions are implemented, so time stress is never permanently reduced. That means lives are spent battling crises 95 per cent of the time and escaping 5 per cent of the time.

A better alternative is to focus on activities in the *Important/Non-urgent* quadrant (Cell 3). These activities might be labelled *opportunities* instead of *problems*. They are oriented toward accomplishing high priority results. They prevent problems from occurring, or build systems that eliminate problems rather than just coping with them. Preparation, preventive maintenance, planning, building resiliency and organising are all 'non-have-to' activities that are crucial for long-term success. Because they are not urgent, however, they often get driven out of managers' time schedules.

Important/Non-urgent activities should be the number one priority on the time management agenda. By making certain that these kinds of activities get priority, the urgent problems being encountered can be reduced. Time stressors can be eliminated.

One of the most difficult yet crucially important decisions one must make in managing time effectively is determining what is important and what is urgent. There are no automatic rules of thumb that divide all activities, demands or opportunities into those neat categories. Problems don't come with an 'Important/ Non-urgent' tag attached. In fact, for each individual, every problem or time demand may hold different degrees of importance. But if managers let others determine what is and is not important, they will never effectively manage their time.

Instead of leaving his appointments diary in the control of his secretary, one chief executive reorganised the way he managed his time by deciding what activities he wanted to accomplish, then allocating specific blocks of time to work on those activities. Only after he had made these decisions did he make his diary available to his secretary to schedule other appointments.

The question still remains, however: How can people make certain that they focus on activities that are important, not just urgent? The answer is to identify clear and specific personal priorities. It is important for people to be aware of their own core values and to establish a set of basic principles to guide their behaviour. In order to determine what is important in time management, those core values, basic principles and personal priorities must be clearly identified. Otherwise, individuals are at the mercy of the unremitting demands that others place upon them.

In order to help you articulate clearly the basis for judging the importance of activities, consider the following questions:

1. What do I stand for? What am I willing to die (or live) for?
2. What do I care passionately about?
3. What legacy would I like to leave? What do I want to be remembered for?
4. If I could persuade everyone in the world to follow a few basic principles, what would they be?
5. What do I want to have accomplished twenty years from now?

Answering these questions can help you create a personal mission statement. A personal mission statement is an articulation of the criteria you use for evaluating what is important. Other people generally help determine what is urgent. But judging importance must be done in relation to a set of personal principles and values.

Two people aged 26 and 56 wrote their Mission Statements. The 26-year-old was concerned with learning new skills so that in four years' time he and his partner could set up a business on their own. The 56-year-old was concerned with her grand children, and passing her skills and the progress she had made in the organisation on to a new generation of managers.

Basing time management on core principles to judge the importance of activities is also the key to being able to say 'no' without feeling guilty. When you have decided what it is that you care about passionately, what it is you most want to accomplish and what legacy you want to leave, you can more easily say 'no' to activities that don't concord with those principles. People frequently say 'no' to something, but usually they are saying 'no' to *Important/Non-urgent activities* (Cell 3) that are most congruent with their personal missions. People who experience the most time stress are those who allow others to generate their personal mission statement for them through their time demands. Making personal core principles precise and public not only helps make them more powerful, but also provides a basis for saying 'no' without feeling guilty. You can opt for prevention, planning, personal development and continuous improvement, knowing that these Important/Non-urgent activities will help eliminate and prevent the problems that create time stress. Effectiveness in time management then means that you accomplish what you want to accomplish with your time. How you achieve those accomplishments relates to efficiency of time use, to which we now turn.

Efficient Time Management

In addition to approaching time management from the point of view of effectiveness (i.e., aligning time use with core personal principles), it is also important to approach time management from the view point of efficiency (i.e., accomplishing more by avoiding wasting time). Techniques are available to help managers utilise more efficiently the time they have each day. One way to enhance efficient time use is to be alert to your own tendencies to use time inefficiently. The list of propositions in Table 4 shows the pitfalls that are commonly encountered for many individuals in their use of time. Sometimes the pitfalls may in fact point towards appropriate responses, but in other circumstances, they can get in the way of efficient time management and increase time stressors unless individuals are aware of them and their possible consequences. For example, if 'we do things that are planned before things that are unplanned', some important tasks may never get done unless consciously scheduled. Because many people have a tendency to 'do things that are urgent before things that are important', they may find themselves saying 'no' to important things in order to attend to urgent things, thereby perpetuating feelings of overload. If 'we do the things that are easiest before the things that are difficult', our time may be taken up dealing with mundane and easy-to-resolve issues while difficult but important problems go unresolved.

Table 4 Potential time management pitfalls

We tend to do:	We respond to:
■ the 'easy' jobs first	■ crisis as opposed to planning ahead
■ the personally rewarding or interesting jobs first	■ things that are politically advisable
■ the shorter jobs first	■ deadlines
■ the scheduled as opposed to the unscheduled	■ things that can be finished in set times
■ what is planned as opposed that which needs planning	■ small jobs and trivia
■ what we do on the basis of WHO needs it and not on real priority	■ the belief that doing something is better than waiting for clarity
■ the urgent and not the most important	■ the 'top of the pile'
	■ the 'squeaky wheel' – the squeaky wheel gets the priority for oiling because it annoys us most

Time is such a universal stressor, and time management is such an effective means for coping with it, that we included in the Pre-assessment section an instrument to help you diagnose your own time management competency – the Time Management Survey. The first section of that survey applies to everyone in their daily life. The second section is most applicable to individuals who have managed or worked in an organisation. The key to scoring is towards the end of the book and will show you how well you manage your time compared with others. The rules set out below cover the basics of effective time management which in turn correspond to the categories of the Time Management Survey – the idea being that you will be able to focus on the rules most applicable to you personally.

The Time Management Survey lists rules of thumb or techniques that have been derived from research. Whereas one kind of time stressor is having too much time available (i.e., boredom), this is not usually the one facing managers and students. These particular rules, therefore, relate to the opposite problem – having too little time available due to an excessive workload.

It should also be pointed out that no individual can or should implement all of these time management techniques at once. The amount of time spent trying to implement all the techniques would be so overwhelming that time stressors would only increase. Therefore, it is best to incorporate a few of these techniques at a time into everyday life. Implement first those hints that will lead to the most improvement in your use of time. Saving just 10 per cent more time, or using an extra thirty minutes a day more wisely can produce astounding results over months and years.

Effective time management then, not only helps a person accomplish more in a typical work day, but also helps eliminate feelings of stress and overload.

The 40 Rules of Effective Time Management
The first 20 rules are applicable to everyone; the second set relate more directly to managers and the management role.

> **Rule 1**   Read selectively. This applies mainly to individuals who find
> themselves with too much material they must read – post,
> magazines, newspapers, books, brochures, instructions and so on.
> Except when you read for relaxation or pleasure, most reading
> should be done the way you read a newspaper; skim most of it, but
> stop to read what seems most important. Even the most important
> articles don't need a thorough reading, since important points are
> generally at the beginnings of paragraphs or sections. Furthermore,

if you underline or highlight what you find important, you can
review it quickly when you need to.

Rule 2   Make a list of things to perform today. This is a common-
sense rule which implies that you need to do some advance
planning each day and not rely solely on your memory. (It also
implies that you should have only one list, not multiple lists on
multiple scraps of paper).

Rule 3   Have a place for everything and keep everything is its place.
Letting things get out of place robs you of time in two ways: you
need more time to find something when you need it, and you are
tempted to interrupt the task you are doing to do something else.
For example, if material for several projects is scattered on top of
your desk, you will be continually tempted to switch from one
project to another as you shift your eyes or move the papers.

Rule 4   Prioritise your tasks. Each day you should focus first on
important tasks, then deal with urgent tasks. During World War II,
with an overwhelming number of tasks to perform, General
Eisenhower successfully managed his time by following Rule 4
strictly. He focused his attention rigorously on important matters
that only he could resolve, while leaving urgent, but less important
matters to be dealt with by subordinates.

Rule 5   Do one important thing at a time but several trivial things
simultaneously. You can accomplish a lot by doing more than one
thing at a time when tasks are routine, trivial or require little
thought. This rule allows managers to get rid of multiple trivial
tasks in less time (e.g., signing letters while talking on the phone).

Rule 6   Make a list of some five- or ten-minute discretionary tasks.
This helps use the small bits of time almost everyone has during his
or her day (waiting for something to begin, between meetings or
events, talking on the telephone, etc.). Beware, however, of
spending all your time doing these small discretionary tasks while
letting high-priority items go unattended.

Rule 7   Divide up large projects. This helps you avoid feeling
overwhelmed by large, important, urgent tasks. Feeling that a task
is too big to accomplish contributes to a feeling of overload and
leads to procrastination.

Rule 8   Determine the critical 20 per cent of your tasks. Pareto's law
states that only 20 per cent of the work produces 80 per cent of the
results. Therefore, it is important to analyse which tasks make up the
most important 20 per cent and spend the bulk of your time on those.

Rule 9 Save your best time for important matters. Time spent on trivial tasks should not be your 'best time'. Do routine work when your energy level is low, your mind is not sharp or you aren't on top of things. Reserve your high-energy time for accomplishing the most important and urgent tasks. As Carlson (1951) pointed out, managers are often like puppets whose strings are being pulled by a crowd of unknown and unorganised people. Don't let others interrupt your best time with unwanted demands. You, not others, should control your time.

Rule 10 Reserve some time during the day when others don't have access to you. Use this time to accomplish Important/Non-urgent tasks, or spend it just thinking. This might be the time before others in the household get up, after everyone else is in bed or at a location where no one else comes. The point is to avoid being in the line of fire all day, every day, without personal control over your time.

Rule 11 Don't put things off. If you do certain tasks promptly, they will require less time and effort than if you procrastinate. Of course, you must guard against spending all your time on trivial, immediate concerns that crowd out more important tasks. The line between procrastination and time wasting is a fine one.

Rule 12 Keep track of time use. This is one of the best time-management strategies. It is impossible to improve your management of time or decrease time stressors unless you know how you spend your time. Your should keep time logs in short enough intervals to capture the essential activities, but not so short that they create a recording burden (e.g., 30 minute periods). Parts of the Skill Practice and Skill Application sections suggest that you keep a time log for at least two weeks. One way to analyse a time log after it is has been recorded is to use the rating scales in Table 5 (next page). Eliminate those activities that consistently receive C's and D's.

Rule 13 Set deadlines. This helps improve your efficient use of time. Work always expands to fill the time available, so if you don't specify a termination time, tasks tend to continue longer than they need to.

Rule 14 Do something productive while waiting. Some estimate that up to 20 per cent of an average person's time is spent in waiting. During such time, try reading, planning, preparing, rehearsing, reviewing, outlining or doing other things that help you accomplish your work.

Table 5 The dimensions of priority

1. IMPORTANCE a) Very important – a must b) Important – should be done c) Not so important but it would be nice if it were done d) Unimportant – no real point in it anyway when you think	**3. DELEGATION** a) I am the only one who can do it b) It can be delegated but requires some authority, training or instruction c) Virtually anyone could do it
2. URGENCY a) Very urgent – must be done NOW b) Urgent – should be done soon c) Not urgent – should be fitted in sometime d) Time is not a factor	**4. INTERACTIONS** a) I must see these people every day b) I need to see these people frequently c) I should see them sometime d) I do not NEED to see these people at all

Rule 15   Do busy work at one set time during the day. Because it is natural to let simple tasks drive out difficult tasks (see Table 5), specify a certain period of time to do busy work. Refusing to answer letters or read the newspaper until a specified time, for example, can help ensure that those activities don't supersede priority time.

Rule 16   Finish at least one thing every day. Reaching the end of a day with nothing completely finished (even a ten-minute task) serves to increase a sense of overload and time stress. Finishing a task, on the other hand, produces a sense of relief and releases stress.

Rule 17   Schedule some personal time. You need some time when no interruptions will occur, when you can get off the 'fast track' for awhile and be alone with yourself. This time should be used to plan, prioritise, take stock, pray, meditate or just relax. Among other advantages, personal time also helps you maintain self-awareness.

Rule 18   Don't worry about anything continually. Allow yourself to worry only at a specified time and avoid dwelling on a worrisome issue at other times. This keeps your mind free and your energy focused on the task at hand.

Rule 19   Have long-term objectives. This helps you maintain consistency in activities and tasks. You can be efficient and organised but still accomplish nothing unless you have a clear direction in mind.

Rule 20 Be on the alert for ways to improve your management of time.

Efficient Time Management for Managers

The second list of rules encompasses the major activities in which managers engage at work. The first nine rules deal with conducting meetings, since managers report that approximately 70 per cent of their time is spent in meetings (Mintzberg, 1973; Cooper and Davidson, 1982).

Rule 1 Hold routine meetings at the end of the day. Energy and creativity levels are highest early in the day and shouldn't be wasted on trivial matters. Furthermore, an automatic deadline (quitting time) will set a time limit on the meeting.

Rule 2 Hold short meetings standing up. This guarantees that meetings will be kept short. Getting comfortable helps prolong meetings.

Rule 3 Set a time limit. This establishes an expectation of when the meeting should end and creates pressure to conform to a time boundary. Set such limits at the beginning of every meeting and appointment.

Rule 4 Cancel meetings once in a while. Meetings should be held only if they are needed. Thus, meetings that are held are more productive and more time efficient.

Rules 5, 6, and 7 Have agendas; stick to them; and keep minutes and time. These rules help people prepare for a meeting, stick to the subject and remain work oriented. Many things will be handled outside of meetings if they have to appear on a formal agenda to be discussed. Managers can set a verbal agenda at the beginning of even impromptu meetings. Keeping a record of the meeting ensures that assignments are not forgotten, that follow-up and accountability occur, and that everyone is clear about expectations.

Rule 8 Start meetings on time. This helps guarantee that people will arrive on time. (Some managers set meetings for odd times, such as 10:13 a.m., to make attendees minute-conscious). People who arrive on time should be rewarded, not asked to wait for laggards.

Rule 9 Prepare minutes promptly and follow them up. This practice keeps items from appearing again in a meeting without having been resolved. It also creates the expectation that most work should be done outside the meeting. Commitments and expectations made public through minutes are more likely to be fulfilled.

Rule 10 Insist that subordinates suggest solutions to problems. Its purpose is to eliminate the tendency towards upward delegation, that is, for subordinates to delegate difficult problems back to managers by asking for their ideas and solutions. It is more efficient for managers to choose among alternatives devised by subordinates than to generate their own.

Rule 11 Meet people who have come to see you in the doorway. This helps managers maintain control of their time by controlling the use of their office space. It is easier to keep a meeting short if you are standing in the doorway rather than sitting in your office.

Rule 12 Go to subordinates' offices. This is useful if it is practical. The advantage is that it helps managers control the length of a meeting by being free to leave. Of course, if managers spend a great deal of time travelling between subordinates' offices, the rule is not practical.

Rule 14 Use telephone technology – re-route your calls when you want time to yourself and thus cut down on interruptions for some part of the day. It is fine if you can get a subordinate to take the calls but if not, swap time with a colleague – they take your calls for one part of the day in exchange for your reciprocation.

Rule 15 Have a place to work uninterrupted. This helps guarantee that when a deadline is near, the manager can concentrate on the task at hand. Trying to get one's mind focused once more on a task or project after interruptions wastes a lot of time. 'Gearing up' is wasteful if done repeatedly.

Rule 16 Do something definite with every piece of paperwork handled. This keeps managers from shuffling the same items over and over. Not infrequently, 'doing something definite' with a piece of paper means throwing it away.

Rule 17 Keep the working space clean. This minimises distractions and reduces the time it takes to find things.

Rules 18, 19, and 20 These relate to effective delegation, a key time-management technique. These last three rules are discussed in the book from the series – *Effective Empowerment and Delegation*.

Remember that these rules of thumb for managing time are a means to an end, not the end itself. If trying to implement rules creates more rather than less stress, they should not be applied. However, research has indicated that managers who use these kinds of techniques have better control of their time, accomplish more, have better relations with subordinates and eliminate many

of the time stressors most managers ordinarily encounter. Therefore, you will find that as you select a few of these hints to apply in
your own life, the efficiency of your time use will improve and
your time stress will decrease.

Most time-management techniques involve single individuals
changing their own work habits or behaviours by themselves.
Greater effectiveness and efficiency in time use occurs because
individuals decide to institute personal changes; the behaviour of
other people is not involved. However, effective time management
must often take into account the behaviour of others, because that
behaviour may tend to inhibit or enhance effective time use. For
this reason, effective time management sometimes requires the
application of other skills discussed in this book. The book from
the series *Effective Empowerment and Delegation*, provides principles for efficient time management by involving other people in
task accomplishment, whilst the book *Effective Motivation* explains
how to help others be more effective and efficient in their own
work. Finally, *Effective Communication* (a further book in this
series) identifies ways in which interpersonal relationships can be
strengthened, thus relieving stressors resulting from interpersonal
conflicts. It is to these encounter stressors that we now turn.

Eliminating Encounter Stressors Through Collaboration and Interpersonal Competence

As pointed out earlier, dissatisfying relationships with others, particularly with a direct manager or supervisor, are prime causes of
job stress among workers. These encounter stressors result directly from abrasive, non-fulfilling relationships. Even though work is
going smoothly, when encounter stress is present, everything else
seems wrong. Life isn't much fun when you're fighting with your
spouse or best friend.

Collaboration

One important factor that helps eliminate encounter stress is
membership in a stable, closely-knit group or community. It was

discovered 25 years ago by Dr. Stewart Wolf that in the town of Roseto, Pennsylvania, residents were completely free from heart disease and other stress-related illness. He suspected that their protection sprang from the town's uncommon social cohesion and stability. The town's population consisted entirely of descendants of Italians who had moved there 100 years ago from Roseto, Italy. Few married outside the community; the firstborn was always named after a grandparent; conspicuous consumption and displays of superiority were avoided; and social support among community members was a way of life.

Wolf predicted that residents would begin to display the same level of stress-related illness as the rest of the country if the modern world intruded. It did, and they did. By the mid-1970s, residents in Roseto had exotic cars, mansion-style homes, mixed marriages, new names, competition with one another and a rate of coronary disease the same as any other town's (Farnham, 1991). They had ceased to be a cohesive, collaborative clan and instead had become a community of selfishness. Self-centredness, it was discovered, was dangerous to health.

The most important psychological discovery resulting from the Vietnam and Persian Gulf Wars was the strength associated with the small, primary work group. In Vietnam, unlike with Desert Storm, strong primary groups of soldiers who stayed together over time were not formed. The constant injection of new personnel into squadrons, and the constant transfer of soldiers from one location to another made soldiers feel isolated, without loyalty and vulnerable to stress-related illness. In the Persian Gulf War, by contrast, soldiers were kept in the same unit throughout the campaign, brought home together and given lots of time to debrief together after the battle. (Farnham, 1991)

Professional debriefing and the use of a closely-knit group to provide interpretation and social support was found to be the most powerful deterrent to post-battle trauma – i.e., Post Traumatic Stress Disorder (PSMS). Woods and Whitehead (1993), give three examples of social support: the restoration of civilian morale in Darmstadt German after one of the most intensive aerial bombardments in the Second World War; the recovery after the flooding and destruction of Les Salles in Southern France; and the acceptance of the horrors of the Bradford Football Stadium fire where 55 people were burnt to death in the sight of their friends. In all these cases the support of tight-knit communities aided recovery.

Developing collaborative, clan-like relationships with others is a powerful deterrent to encounter stress. One way of developing this kind of relationship is by applying a concept introduced by Stephen Covey (1989) in describing habits of highly effective people. Covey used the metaphor of an emotional bank account to describe the trust or feeling of security that one person has toward another. The more 'deposits' made in an emotional bank account, the stronger and more resilient the relationship becomes. Conversely, too many 'withdrawals' from the account weakens relationships by destroying trust, security and confidence. 'Deposits' are made through treating people with kindness, courtesy, honesty and consistency. The emotional bank account grows when people feel they are receiving love, respect and caring. 'Withdrawals' are made by not keeping promises, not listening, not clarifying expectations or allowing choice. Because disrespect and autocratic rule devalue people and destroy a sense of self-worth, relationships are ruined because the account becomes overdrawn.

The more people interact, the more deposits must be made in the emotional bank account. When you see an old friend after years of absence, you can often pick up right where you left off, because the emotional bank account has not been touched. But when you interact with someone frequently, the relationship is constantly being fed or depleted. Cues from everyday interactions are interpreted as either deposits or withdrawals. When the emotional account is well-stocked, mistakes, disappointments and minor abrasions are easily forgiven and ignored. But when no reserve exists, those incidents may become creators of distrust and contention.

The common-sense prescription, therefore, is to base relationships with others on mutual trust, respect, honesty and kindness. Make deposits into the emotional bank accounts of others. Collaborative, cohesive communities are, in the end, a product of the one-on-one relationships that people develop with each other. As Dag Hammarskjold, former Secretary General of the United Nations, stated: 'It is more noble to give yourself completely to one individual than to labour diligently for the salvation of the masses'. That is because building a strong, cohesive, relationship with an individual is more powerful, and more difficult, than the leadership of masses.

Feeling trusted, respected and loved is, in the end, what each of us desires as individuals. We want to experience those feelings personally, not just as a member of a group. Therefore, because encounter stressors are almost always the product of abrasive individual relationships, they are best eliminated by building strong emotional bank accounts with individuals.

Interpersonal Competence

In addition to one-on-one relationship building, a second major category of encounter stress eliminators is developing *interpersonal competence*. The skilful management of groups and interpersonal interactions is also an effective way to eliminate encounter stressors. For example, the ability to resolve conflict; to build and manage high performing teams; to conduct efficient meetings; to coach and counsel employees needing support; to provide negative feedback in constructive ways; to influence others' opinions; to motivate and energise employees; and to empower individuals on the job, all help eliminate the stress associated with abrasive, uncomfortable relationships. A survey of workers found that employees who rated their manager as supportive and interpersonally competent had lower rates of burnout, lower stress levels, lower incidence of stress-related illness, higher productivity, more loyalty to their organisations, and more efficiency in work than employees with non-supportive and interpersonally incompetent managers.

The other books in this series address these topics in detail. They provide techniques and behavioural guidelines designed to assist you in improving your interpersonal competence. Thus, after completing the book – including the practice and application exercises – you will have improved several skills related to interpersonal competence and, therefore, your ability to eliminate many forms of encounter stress.

Eliminating Situational Stressors Through Work Redesign

Most people would never admit that they feel less stress now than a year ago; that they have less pressure; that they are less overloaded. Most people report feeling stress because it is seems fashionable to be stressed. 'I'm busier than you are' is a common theme in social conversations. We discuss the problems of repeated reorganisations and the vulnerability of all 'our' jobs; the traffic jams in the cities; the difficulties in establishing rights; and the law and order problem, often relating it directly or indirectly to our own stresses. Unfortunately, in medical treatment and time lost, stress-related illness are almost twice as expensive as workplace injuries because of longer recovery times and the need for expensive therapy (Farnham, 1991). Situational stressors, in other words, are costly and they are escalating.

For decades, researchers in the area of occupational health have examined the relationship between job strain and stress-related behavioural, psychological and physiological outcomes. Studies have focused on various components of job strain, including the level of task demand (e.g., the pressure to work quickly or excessively), the level of individual control (e.g., the freedom to vary the work pace), and the level of intellectual challenge (e.g., the extent to which work is interesting).

The kind of stress experienced by individuals will vary according to their culture. In a study by Cary Cooper *et al.*, (1988) of nearly 1,000 senior top level executives in ten countries it was found that each country presents its own idiosyncratic work pressures. Cooper also looked specifically at the stresses of women managers.

U.S. executives perceive their greatest source of pressure at work to be 'the lack of power and influence', 'incompetent bosses' and 'beliefs conflicting with those of the organisation'. However,

Japanese executives rated 'keeping up with new technology' as their major source of strain and job dissatisfaction, while Swedish executives cited stresses involving encroachment of work upon their private lives. German complaints were more specific; they complained of 'time pressures' and 'working with inadequately trained subordinates'.

Other research in this area however, has challenged the common myth that job strain occurs most frequently in the executive suite (Hingley and Cooper 1986). In a General Household Survey 1974–75, the frequency of deaths due to major causes increases as we move from professional and white collar jobs down to the unskilled. This applies both to stress-related illness and to other illness' such as pneumonia and prostrate cancer. Many blue collar workers show a greater number of restricted activity days and consultation with GP's than do white collar workers in the UK. Professional males average 12 days restricted activity per year, while unskilled manual workers average around 20 days. An explanation for this could well be that low discretion, low interest jobs with high demand produce at least as much as stress as high profile work – a fact that is born out by research.

A review of this research suggests that the single most important contributor to stress is lack of freedom (Adler, 1989). In a study of administrators, engineers and scientists at the Goddard Space Flight Centre, researchers found that individuals provided with more discretion in making decisions about assigned tasks experienced fewer time stressors (e.g., role overload), situational stressors (e.g., role ambiguity), encounter stressors (e.g., interpersonal conflict) and anticipatory stressors (e.g., job-related threats). Individuals without discretion and participation experienced significantly more stress (French and Caplan, 1972).

In response to these findings, Hackman and his colleague (1975) proposed a model of job redesign that has proved effective in reducing stress and in increasing satisfaction and productivity. A detailed discussion of their job redesign model is provided in the book entitled *Effective Motivation*. Here we shall merely outline their remedies for stress-producing job strain.

1. **Combine tasks.** When individuals are able to work on a whole project and perform a variety of related tasks (e.g., programming all components of a computer software package), rather than being restricted to working on a single repetitive task or sub-component of a larger task, they are more satisfied and committed. In such cases, they are able to use more skills and feel a certain pride of ownership in their job.

2. **Form identifiable work units.** Building on the first step, individuals feel more integrated, productivity improves and the strain associated with repetitive work is diminished when teams of individuals performing related tasks are formed. When these groups combine and co-ordinate their tasks, deciding internally how to complete the work, stress decreases dramatically. This formation of natural work units has received a great deal of attention in Japanese auto plants in America and the UK as workers have combined in teams to assemble an entire car from start to finish, rather than do separate tasks on an assembly line. Workers learn one another's jobs, rotate assignments and experience a sense of completion in their work.

3. **Establish customer relationships.** One of the most enjoyable parts of a job is seeing the consequences of one's labour. In most organisations, producers are buffered from consumers by intermediaries, such as customer relations departments and sales personnel. Eliminating those buffers allows workers to obtain first-hand information concerning customer satisfaction as well as the needs and expectations of potential customers. Stress resulting from filtered communication is also eliminated.

4. **Increase decision-making authority.** Managers who increase the autonomy of their subordinates to make important work decisions eliminate a major source of job stress for them. Being able to influence the what, when and how of work increases an individual's feelings of control. Cameron, Freeman, and Mishra (1990) found a significant decrease in experienced stress in firms that were downsizing when workers were given authority to make decisions about how and when they did the extra work required of them.

5. **Open feedback channels.** A major source of stress is not knowing what is expected and how task performance is being evaluated. As managers communicate their expectations more clearly, giving timely and accurate feedback, subordinates' satisfaction and performance improve. A related form of feedback in production tasks is quality control. Firms that allow the individuals who assemble a product to test its quality, instead of shipping it off to a separate quality assurance group, find that quality increases substantially and that conflicts between production and quality control personnel are eliminated.

These practices are used widely today in all types of organisations, such as Volvo, Saab and Philips Industries. They have all undertaken extended projects of job redesign. Philips have pursued a programme of work structuring. Job enrichment and job enlargement have been attempted and greater opportunities for worker participation have been provided.

Eliminating Anticipatory Stressors Through Prioritising, Goal Setting and Small Wins

While redesigning work can help structure an environment where stressors are minimised, it is much more difficult to eliminate entirely the anticipatory stressors experienced by individuals. Stress associated with anticipating an event is more a product of psychological anxiety than current work circumstances. To eliminate that source of stress requires a change in thought processes, priorities and plans. As we have said earlier, it is important to establish clear personal priorities, such as identifying what is to be accomplished in the long-term; what cannot be compromised or sacrificed; and what lasting legacy one desires. Establishing this statement of basic personal principles helps eliminate not only time stressors, but also eliminates anticipatory stress by providing clarity of direction. When travelling on an unknown road for the first time, having a road map reduces anticipatory stress. You don't have to work out where to go or where you are by trying to diagnose the unknown landmarks along the roadside. In the same way, a personal mission statement acts as a map or guide. It makes clear where you will eventually end up. Fear of the unknown – or anticipatory stress – is thus eliminated.

Goal Setting

Establishing short-term plans also help eliminate anticipatory stressors by focusing attention on immediate goal accomplishment instead of a fearful future. Short-term planning, however, implies more than just specifying a desired outcome. Several action steps are needed if short-term plans are to be achieved. The model in Figure 4 outlines the four-step process associated with successful short-term planning.

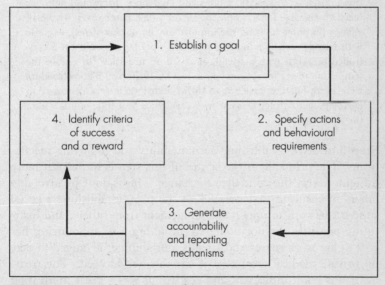

FIGURE 4   A model for short-term planning and goal setting

Step 1 is to identify the desired goal. Most goal-setting, performance appraisal or management-by-objectives (MBO) programs specify that step, but most also stop at that point.

Unfortunately, the first step alone is not likely to lead to goal achievement or stress elimination. Merely establishing a goal, while helpful, is not sufficient. Steps 2, 3, and 4 are also essential.

Step 2 is to identify, as specifically as possible, the activities and behaviours that will lead towards accomplishing the goal. The more difficult the goal is to accomplish, the more rigorous, numerous and specific should be the behaviours and activities.

> A friend approached one of us with a problem. She was a sensitive, single woman about 25 years old who had a high degree of anticipatory stress problem because of her size. She weighed well over 300 pounds and seemed to be unable to lose any of it. She was concerned both from the health and the social consequences of her size. She set a goal, or short-term plan, to lose 100 pounds in the next ten months. Because it was to be such a difficult goal to reach, however, we helped her identify a dozen or so specific actions and guidelines that would help her reach that goal — for example, never eat alone, never carry any small change (in order to avoid the impulse buying of chocolates), exercise with friends each evening in a gym, get up 7:00 a.m. and eat a controlled breakfast with a friend, cut back on television (to reduce the temptation to eat snacks) and go to bed by 10:30 p.m. The behaviours were rigid, but the goal was so difficult that they were necessary to ensure progress. Success came with a weight loss of 100 pounds within the ten months.

Step 3 involves establishing accountability and reporting mechanisms. The principle at the centre of this step is to make it more difficult to stay the same than to change. This is done by involving others in ensuring that we stick to the plan, establishing a social support network to obtain encouragement from others, and instituting penalties for not doing so. In addition to announcing her goal to her work-mates and friends, our slimmer arranged to take up private medical treatment if she did not succeed. The treatment was both unpleasant and costly, but was a great motivating factor to success by nicer means.

Step 4 is establishing an evaluation and reward system. What evidence will there be that the goal has been accomplished? In the case of losing weight, it's just getting on the scales. But for improving management skills, developing more patience,

Table 6 The SMART strategy

Goal	Improve manage- ment skills	Become more patient	Becoming a better leader	*Reader's goal*
Specific	Learn and practice running meetings	Learn to listen more effectively	Give instructions of a project to a subordinate	
Measurable	Reduce the business carried forward to the next meeting to two items	Get a friend to watch you in an interview – aim to speak not more than 30% of the time	Reduce the number of times he or she needs to return to you for clarification to once a week	
Agreed	Check with those attending the meeting	Check with a friend that 30% sounds right – you are now at 80%	Explain the goal to the subordinate	
Realistic	Reduction to two items is fine – no carry forward would be unrealistic	30% is realistic from what you have read	Now we have continuous seeking of clarification – old habits die hard – once a week allows some latitude	
Timed	Our next meeting is on Friday – the plan will start then and be in action on Friday week	The next difficult meeting you will work from 80% to 60% and then by three meetings you will achieve the 30%	This is a real project with real time scales. At the end of its run – three months – we will have success	

establishing more effective leadership, and so on, the criteria of success are not so easily identified. That is why this step is crucial. 'I'll know it when I see it' isn't good enough. Our objectives must be SMART (see Table 6) – specific, measurable, agreed, realistic and timed. For our slimmer, the specific goal was to lose weight 100 pounds and this was agreed by her, her doctor and her friends. The weight loss was realistic, whereas 200 pounds would not have been, and the time scale of ten months (in fact by Christmas) was set. The key is making the goal specific and the purpose is to eliminate anticipatory stress by establishing a focus and direction for activity. The anxiety associated with uncertainty and potentially negative events is dissipated when mental and physical energy are concentrated on purposeful activity.

Small Wins

Turning the vague goal to a specific goal can be described as a *small wins strategy*. By 'small win', we mean a tiny but definite change made in a desired direction. One begins by changing something that is relatively easy to change. Then another 'easy change' is added, and so on. The manager with the meeting problem may want to reduce the carried forward items to zero, but that is not realistic for the first go. Reducing them to two is a small improvement, but it is achievable. In general, each individual success may be relatively modest when considered in isolation, but the small gains mount up and show measurable progress. The progress we see helps convince ourselves, as well as others, of our ability to accomplish our objective. The fear associated with anticipatory change is eliminated as we build self-confidence through small wins. We also gain the support of others as they see things are happening.

In the case of our overweight friend, one key was to begin changing what she could change, a little at a time. Tackling the loss of 100 pounds all at once would have been too overwhelming a task. But she could change the time she shopped, the time she went to bed and what she ate for breakfast. Each successful change generated more and more momentum that, when combined together, led to the larger change that she desired. Her ultimate success was a product of multiple small wins.

Similarly, Weick (1993) has described Poland's peaceful transition from a communistic command economy to a capitalistic free-enterprise economy as a product of small wins. Not only is Poland now one of the most thriving economies in eastern Europe, but it made the change to free enterprise without a single shot being fired, a single strike being called or a single political upheaval. One reason for this is that long before the Berlin Wall fell, small groups of volunteers in Poland began to change the way they lived. They adopted a theme that went something like this:

If you value freedom, then behave freely; if you value honesty, then speak honestly; if you desire change, then change what you can. Polish citizens organised volunteer groups to help at local hospitals, assist the less fortunate and clean up the parks. They behaved in a way that was outside the control of the central government, but reflected their free choice. Their changes were not on a large enough scale to attract attention and official opposition from the central government. But their actions nevertheless reflected their determination to behave in a free, self-determining way. They controlled what they could control, namely, their own voluntary service. These voluntary service groups spread throughout Poland; thus, when the transition from communism to capitalism occurred, a large number of people in Poland had already got used to behaving in a way consistent with self-determination. Many of these people simply stepped into positions where independent-minded managers were needed. The transition was smooth because of the multiple small wins that had previously spread throughout the country relatively unnoticed.

In summary, the rules for instituting small wins are simple:
- Identify something that is under your control
- Change it in a way that leads toward your desired goal
- Find some other small thing to change, and change it
- Keep track of the changes you are making
- Maintain the small gains you have made.

Anticipatory stressors are eliminated because the fearful unknown is replaced by a focus on immediate successes.

Developing Resilience

Some stress cannot be eliminated. People vary widely in their ability to cope with stress: some individuals seem to crumble under pressure, while others appear to thrive. A major predictor of which individuals cope well with stress and which do not is the amount of resilience that they have developed. Resilience is associated with balancing the various aspects of one's life.

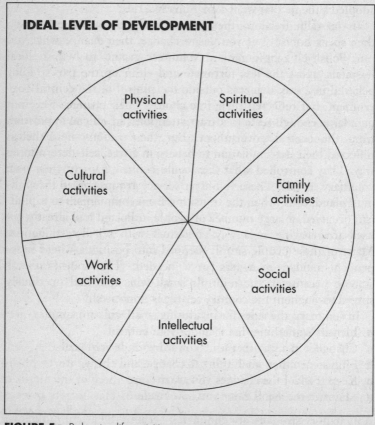

IDEAL LEVEL OF DEVELOPMENT

Physical activities

Spiritual activities

Cultural activities

Family activities

Work activities

Social activities

Intellectual activities

FIGURE 5   Balancing life activities

Assume that the wheel in Figure 5 represents resilience development. Each wedge in the figure identifies an important aspect of life that must be developed in order to achieve resilience. The most resilient individuals are those who have achieved life balance. For example, if the centre of the figure represents the zero point of resilience development and the outside edge of the figure represents maximum development, shading in a portion of the area in each wedge would represent the amount of development achieved in each area. (This exercise is included in the Skill Practice section, page 82). Individuals who are best able to cope with stress would shade in a majority of each wedge, indicating they have not only spent time developing a variety of aspects of their lives, but also that the overall pattern is relatively balanced. A lopsided pattern is as non-adaptive as are minimally shaded areas. Either pattern suggests that an individual who cannot eliminate stressors should seek to develop resilience through life balance.

This is, of course, a counter-intuitive prescription. Generally, when people are feeling stress in one area of life, such as work, they respond by devoting more time and attention to it. While this is a natural reaction, it is counterproductive for several reasons. First, the more that individuals concentrate exclusively on work, the more restricted and less creative they become. As we shall see in the discussion of creativity in the book from the series – *Effective Problem-Solving* – many breakthroughs in problem solving come from using analogies and metaphors gathered from unrelated activities. That is why several major corporations send senior managers on high adventure wilderness retreats (John Scully 1989); invite actors to perform plays before the executive committee; require volunteer community service; or encourage their managers to engage in completely unrelated activities outside of work (Business Week, Sept. 30, 1985, p. 80–84).

Secondly, refreshed and relaxed minds think better. A bank executive commented recently during an executive development workshop that he has gradually become convinced of the merits of taking the weekend off from work. He finds that he gets twice as much accomplished on Monday as his colleagues who have been in their offices all weekend.

Thirdly, the cost of stress-related illness decreases markedly when employees are able to receive support from occupational health services. People need to be able obtain unbiased advice, within their place of work on stress related problems. (Woods and Whitehead, 1993)

Well-developed individuals, who give time and attention to cultural, physical, spiritual, family, social and intellectual activities in addition to work, are more productive and less stressed than those who are workaholics.

In this section, therefore, we concentrate on three common areas of resilience development for managers – physical resilience, psychological resilience and social resilience. Development in each of these areas requires initiative on the part of the individual and takes a moderate amount of time to achieve. These are not activities that can be accomplished by lunch-time or the weekend. Rather, achieving life balance and resilience requires ongoing initiative and continuous effort. Components of resilience are summarised in Table 7.

Table 7   Resiliency: moderating the effects of stress

PHYSIOLOGICAL RESILIENCY
- Cardiovascular conditioning
- Proper diet

PSYCHOLOGICAL RESILIENCY
- Balanced lifestyle
- Hardy personality
  High internal control
  Strong personal commitment
  Love of challenge
- Small-wins strategy
- Deep-relaxation techniques

SOCIAL RESILIENCY
- Supportive social relations
- Mentors
- Teamwork

Physiological Resilience

One of the most crucial aspects of resilience development involves one's physical condition, because physical condition significantly affects the ability to cope with stress. Two aspects of physical condition combine to determine physical resilience: cardiovascular conditioning and dietary control.

Cardiovascular Conditioning

Henry Ford is reputed to have stated, 'Exercise is bunk. If you are healthy, you don't need it. If you are sick, you shouldn't take it'. Fortunately, European business has not taken Ford's advice; thousands of major corporations now have in-house fitness facilities. An emphasis on physical conditioning in business has resulted partly from overwhelming evidence that individuals in good physical condition are better able to cope with stressors than those in poor physical condition. Table 8 shows the benefits of regular physical exercise.

Table 8 Confirmed benefits of regular vigorous exercise (Source: Goldberg, 1978)

- Blood pressure is lowered.
- Resting heart rate is lowered; the heart is better able to distribute blood where needed under stress.
- Cardiac output is increased; the heart is better able to distribute blood where needed under stress.
- Number of red blood cells is increased; more oxygen can be carried per quart of blood.
- Elasticity of arteries is increased.
- Triglyceride level is lowered.
- Blood cholesterol level is decreased. High-density cholesterol, which is more protective of blood vessels than low-density cholesterol, is proportionately increased.
- Adrenal secretions in response to emotional stress are lowered.
- Lactic acid is more efficiently eliminated from the muscles. (This has been associated with decreased fatigue and tension.)
- Fibrin, a protein that aids in the formation of blood clots, is decreased.
- Additional routes of blood supply are built up in the heart.

Marks & Spencer, well known for its work in this area, is one of the founder members of the Wellness Forum. One of the examples of care they give their employees is the provision of oral cancer screening. As a result of its Live for Life programme, Johnson and Johnson lowered absenteeism and sickness cost to produce a saving of about £160 per employee in 1982. Prudential Life Insurance found a 46 per cent reduction in major medical expenses over five years resulting from a workplace fitness programme. The advantages of physical conditioning, both for individuals and for companies, are irrefutable.

Three primary purposes exist for a regular exercise programme: maintaining optimal weight, increasing psychological well-being and improving the cardiovascular system. One indirect cause of stress is the sedentary lifestyle adopted by many individuals. An office worker burns up only about 1200 calories during an eight-hour day. That is fewer calories than are contained in the typical office worker's lunch. It is little wonder that many people are overweight. The resulting excessive strain on both the heart and the self-image makes overweight individuals more vulnerable to stress (Wolman, 1982).

An advantage of regular physical exercise is that it improves mental as well as physical outlook. It increases self-esteem and gives individuals the energy to be more alert and attentive throughout the day. Episodes of depression are far less frequent. Exercise fosters the necessary energy to cope with the stresses of both unexpected events and dull routine. Physically active individuals are less prone to anxiety, have less illness and miss fewer days of work (Griest *et al.*, 1979). Researchers have found a chemical basis for the psychological benefit of exercise: the brain releases endorphins (similar to morphine) during periods of intense physical activity. This substance numbs pain and produces a feeling of well-being, sometimes referred to as 'jogger's high' – a euphoric, relaxed feeling reported by long-distance runners.

Another vital benefit of exercise is a strengthened cardiovascular system (Greenberg, 1987). The best results come from aerobic exercises that do not require more oxygen than a person can take in comfortably (as compared with all-out sprinting or long-distance swimming). This type of exercise includes brisk walking, jogging, riding a bicycle or climbing stairs. However, the cardiovascular system is improved by exercise only when the following

two conditions are met:
1. The target heart rate is sustained throughout the exercise. This rate is 60–80 per cent of the heart's maximum. To work your target rate, subtract your age in years from 220, then take 60–80 per cent of that number. You should begin your exercise programme at the 60 per cent level and gradually increase to the 80 per cent rate. To check your heart rate during your exercise, periodically monitor your heart beat for six seconds and multiply by ten.
2. The exercise should be for 20–30 minutes, three or four time a week. Since cardiovascular endurance decreases after forty-eight hours, it is important to exercise at least every other day.

Dietary Control
The adage 'You are what you eat' is sobering, especially given the fact that Americans who are often seen as trend setters into bad habits, annually consume an average of 100 pounds of refined sugar, 125 pounds of fat, 36 gallons of carbonated beverages, and 25 times more salt than the human body requires (Perl, 1980). Europeans, however, do seem to be eating a more healthy diet and Government programmes throughout the EC are encouraging this. After years of attack by health professionals in magazines, newspapers, books and TV programmes, old eating habits are finally being swept away. It is now clearly understood that good diet is linked to good health. A healthy diet need not be hard work, a few simple changes can soon put you on the right road:

- Reduce the total amount of fat you eat especially saturated fats, and partially replace with polyunsaturated fats. Eat more fresh fish, lean meat and poultry, rather than high saturated fat foods such as sausages and burgers.
- Increase your intake of fibre-rich starchy foods, such as wholemeal bread and pasta, baked jacket potatoes, high fibre breakfast cereals, oats and pulses.
- Eat plenty of fresh fruit and vegetables.
- Cut down on your sugar by opting for unsweetened fruit juices or low calorie soft drinks and eating less sugary foods such as cakes, puddings, sweets and biscuits.

■ Limit the quantity of salt you take by using less in cooking and at the table and by eating fresh fruit instead of salty crisps and nuts – which are also high in fat.

(Source: The Flora Project for Heart Disease Prevention)

Psychological Resilience

Another important moderator of the effects of stress is an individual's psychological resilience. Individuals with certain psychological characteristics, sometimes referred to as 'personality types', tend to handle stress better than others. We will focus especially on two examples that show best the relationship between personality and vulnerability to stress: the Hardy personality and the Type A personality. First we will introduce the concept of 'hardiness' and use it to discuss general psychological attributes that foster resilience. Then we will focus on three stress-prone elements of the Type A personality and outline techniques for eliminating them.

Hardiness

In their book, *The Hardy Executive*, Maddi and Kobasa (1984) described three elements that characterise a hardy, or highly stress-resistant, personality. Hardiness results from:

■ Feeling in control of one's life, rather than powerless to shape external events

■ Feeling committed to and involved in what one is doing, rather than alienated from one's work and other individuals

■ Feeling challenged by new experiences rather than viewing change as a threat to security and comfort.

According to these authors, hardy individuals tend to interpret stressful situations positively and optimistically, responding to stress constructively. As a result, their incidence of illness and emotional dysfunction under stressful conditions is considerably below the norm.

Three concepts – **control, commitment and challenge** – are central to the development of a variety of management skills, and are crucial for mitigating the harmful effects of stress (Kobasa,

1982). Individuals with a high degree of internal control feel that they are in charge of their own destinies. They take responsibility for their actions and feel they can neutralise negative external forces. They generally believe that stressors are the result of their personal choices rather than uncontrollable, capricious or even malicious external forces. The belief that one can influence the course of events is central to developing high self-esteem. Self-esteem, in turn, engenders self-confidence and the optimistic view that bad situations can be improved and problems overcome. Confidence in one's own efficacy produces low fear of failure, high expectations, willingness to take risks and persistence under adversity (Mednick, 1982; Anderson, 1977; Ivancevich and Matteson, 1980), all of which contribute to resilience under stress.

Commitment implies both selection and dedication. Hardy individuals not only feel that they choose what they do, but they also strongly believe in the importance of what they do. This commitment is both internal (that is, applied to one's own activities) and external (that is, applied to a larger community). The feeling of being responsible to others is an important buffer against stress (Antonovsky, 1979). Whereas self-esteem and a sense of purpose help provide a psychological support system for coping with stressful events, an individual's belief that others are counting on him or her to succeed, and that he or she belongs to a larger community, fosters psychological resilience during stressful periods. Feeling part of a group, cared about and trusted by others engender norms of co-operation and commitment, and encourage constructive responses to stress.

Hardy people also welcome challenge. They believe that change, rather than stability, is the normal and preferred mode of life. Therefore, much of the disruption associated with a stressful life event is interpreted as an opportunity for personal growth rather than as a threat to security. This mode of thinking is consistent with the Chinese word for crisis, which has two meanings: 'threat' and 'opportunity'. Individuals who seek challenges search for new and interesting experiences and accept stress as a necessary step toward learning. Because these individuals prefer change over stability, they tend to have high tolerance for ambiguity and high resilience under stress (Ivancevich and Matteson, 1980; Maddi and Kobasa, 1984). The three characteristics of hardy personalities – control, commitment and challenge – have been found to be among the most powerful ways of reducing the dysfunctional consequences of stress. By contrast, a different complex of personality attributes, the so-called 'Type A Syndrome', is associated with reduced hardiness and higher levels of psychological stress.

The Type A Personality

A second important aspect of psychological resilience relates to a personality pattern many individuals develop as they enter the competitive worlds of advanced education and management. By far the most well-known connection between personality and resilience relates to a combination of attributes known as the *Type A personality*. For at least three decades scientists have been aware of a link between certain personality attributes and stress-related behavioural, psychological and physiological problems such as anxiety, deteriorating relationships and heart disease (Friedman and Rosenman, 1959). Table 9 summarises the primary attributes of Type A personalities that have emerged from the research.

Table 9   Characteristics of the Type A personality

- Signs of personal tension, such as a clenched jaw, tight muscles, tics.
- Personal commitment to having, rather than being.
- Unawareness of the broader environment. Ignorance of elements outside the immediate task.
- Strong need to be an expert on a subject; otherwise, lack of involvement.
- Compulsion to compete with other Type A's rather than understanding and cooperate with them.
- Speech characterized by explosive accentuation, acceleration of the last few words of a sentence, impatience when interrupted.
- Chronic sense of being in a hurry.

- Polyphasic thoughts and actions, that is, a tendency to do several things simultaneously.
- Impatience with the normal pace of events. Tendency to finish others' sentences.
- Doing everything rapidly.
- Feelings of guilt when relaxing.
- Tendency to evaluate all activities in terms of measurable results.
- Belief that Type A attributes are what lead to ssuccess.
- Frequent knee-jiggling or finger-tapping.
- Determination to win every game, even when playing with those who are less skilled or experienced.

The manner in which Friedman and Rosenman, both cardiologists, discovered the link between personality and heart disease is intriguing. Observing that their waiting room was becoming a bit shabby, they decided to have their chairs re-upholstered. The decorator pointed out that only the front edges of the chairs were worn. The doctors suddenly realised that their patients seemed to be 'on edge', literally sitting on the edges of their seats, prepared for action.

Following up their observations with intensive interviews, they noted that during interviews, many of their patients showed signs of impatience and hostility such as fidgeting, eye-blinking, grimaces, rapid or explosive speech, interrupting, and filling in incomplete sentences during a pause. The opposite personality types – which they labelled Type B – appeared more relaxed, patient and able to listen without interrupting. Over 15 per cent of Friedman and Rosenman's Type A patient had had heart attacks, compared to seven per cent of Type B's.

Subsequent research has found that in America about 70 per cent of men and 50 per cent of women exhibit Type A personality traits, such as extreme competitiveness, strong desires for achievement, haste, impatience, restlessness, hyper-alertness, explosive speech, tenseness of facial muscles, free-floating hostility and so on. Rosenman suggested that anger, impatience and competitiveness were the most debilitating factors in the Type A personality; others have proposed hostility (Greenberg, 1987); and some have blamed a feeling of urgency that keeps adrenaline constantly flowing (Kobasa, 1979). Regardless of the key ingredient, the Type A personality is certain to have a disastrous effect on well-being.

In the most extensive study of personality effects on heart disease ever conducted, an eight-year survey of 3,400 men found that Type A individuals in the 39–49-year age group had approximately 6·5 times the likelihood of heart disease as Type B's. Even when factors such as cigarette smoking, parental medical history, blood pressure and cholesterol levels were taken into account, the Type A personality still accounted for two to three times greater likelihood of heart disease. This research concluded that personality is a better predictor than physiology of cardiovascular illness

(Friedman and Rosenman, 1974). Ironically, subsequent research has also found that whereas Type A personalities are more prone to experience heart attacks, they are also more likely to recover from them.

Most Type A individuals believe that it is their Type A personality that has led to their success. Many are unwilling to give up that orientation because hard-driving, intense, persistent action is generally admired and valued among managers. This has often been associated with the traditional male management role, but it has also been connected to the disproportionately high incidence of heart disease among men. In fact, Goldberg (1976) and Jourard (1964) initially linked Type A personality characteristics to certain sex-linked behaviour patterns.

Specifically, males or females who followed stereotypic views of appropriate male behaviour were found to be more likely to experience stress-related illness. They tended to equate low self-disclosure, low emotional involvement, low display of feelings, high defensiveness and high insensitivity to the acquisition of power and control – the presumed prerequisites for success. These were so typical of male behaviour in the workplace that they became known as 'the lethal aspects of the male role' (Jourard, 1964). As more women began to enter the work force, this same pattern became less and less gender-linked. Many women also behaved as if acceptance in the workplace required 'acting as masculine' i.e., as their male counterparts. As a result, the gap between stress-related illness among professional men and women has narrowed. In recent years, female stress-related illness (e.g., heart attacks, suicides, migraine headaches) has actually surpassed those of males in some professions. This trend is not only tragic but ironic, because corporations are spending huge amounts each year on training workshops designed to encourage their managers to become more sensitive, understanding and supportive. The folly of the Type A approach to management – and to life – is illustrated in the following story from the lore of Zen Buddhism.

Matajura wanted to become a great swordsman, but his father said he wasn't quick enough and could never learn. So Matajura went to the famous dueller, Banzo, and asked to become his pupil. 'How long will

it take me to become a master?' he asked. 'Suppose I become your ser-
vant, and spend every minute with you; how long?'

'Ten years.' said Banzo.

'My father is getting old. Before ten years have passed, I will have
to return home to take care of him. Suppose I work twice as hard; how
long will it take me?'

'Thirty years.' said Banzo.

'How is that?' asked Matajura. 'First you say ten years. Then when
I offer to work twice as hard, you say it will take three times as long.
Let me make myself clear: I will work unceasingly; no hardship will be
too much. How long will it take?'

'Seventy years.' said Banzo. 'A pupil in such a hurry learns slowly.'

This Type A sense of urgency, of being able to overcome any
obstacle by working harder and longer, works against the ability to
develop psychological hardiness. When stressors are encountered,
arousal levels increase, and the tendency is to combat them by
increasing arousal levels or effort even further. But at high
arousal levels, coping responses become more primitive (Staw,
Sandelands and Dutton, 1981). Patterns of response that were
learned most recently are the first ones to disappear, which means
that the responses that are most finely tuned to the current stressful situation are the first ones to go. The ability to distinguish
among fine-grained stimuli actually deteriorates, so the extra
energy expended by individuals trying to cope becomes less and
less effective. Weick (1984) pointed out that highly stressed
people consequently find it difficult to learn new responses, to
brainstorm, to concentrate, to resist relying on old non-adaptive
behaviour patterns, to perform complex responses, to delegate
and to avoid the vicious spiral of escalating arousal. Resilience
deteriorates.

The Small-Wins Strategy

An effective antidote to this Type A escalation problem is working
for 'small wins', as discussed earlier. When individuals work for
small wins, they consciously remain sensitive to their small successes – and celebrate them – while coping with a major stressor.

A hypothetical example introduced by Kuhn and Beam (1982,
p. 249-250) illustrates the power of small wins:

Your task is to count out a thousand sheets of paper while you are subject to periodic interruptions. Each interruption causes you to lose track of the count and forces you to start over. If you count the thousand as a single sequence, then an interruption could cause you to lose count of as many as 999. If the sheets are put into stacks of 100, however, and each stack remains undisturbed by interruptions, then the worst possible count loss from interruption is 108. That number represents the recounting of nine stacks of 100 each plus 99 single sheets. Further, if sheets are first put into stacks of ten, which are then joined into stacks of 100, the worst possible loss from interruption would be 27. That number represents nine stacks of 100 plus nine stacks of ten plus nine single sheets. Not only is far less recounting time lost by putting the paper into 'subsystems' of tens and hundreds, but the chances of completing the count are vastly higher.

When individuals work for a small, concrete outcome (giving them a chance to enjoy visible success), heightened confidence, excitement and optimism result which motivates an attempt to accomplish another small win. By itself, a small win may seem unimportant. A series of wins at seemingly insignificant tasks, however, reveals a pattern that tends to attract allies, deter opponents and lower resistance to further action. Once a small win has been accomplished, forces are set in motion that favour another small win. When one solution has been identified, the next solvable problem often becomes more visible. Additional resources also tend to flow toward winners, so the probability of additional successes increases.

Research clearly demonstrates that a small-wins strategy is superior to a strategy of trying to cope with stressors in large chunks. For example, successive small requests are more likely to be approved and achieve compliance than one large request (Freedman and Fraser, 1966). Positions advocated within the latitude of acceptance (i.e., that are only slightly different from current positions) modify opinions more than does advocacy of a position that exceeds those limits (i.e., large differences exist between current and proposed positions). People whose positions are close to one's own tend to be the targets of the most intensive persuasion attempts, while those whose positions are farther away are dismissed, isolated or derogated.

Cognitive therapy is most successful when the patient is persuaded to do just one thing differently that changes his or her pattern of coping up to that point. Learning tends to occur in small increments rather than in large, all-or-nothing chunks. Retention of learning is better when individuals are in an emotional state similar to the one in which they learned the original material. Over 75 per cent of the changes and improvements in both individuals and organisations over time can be accounted for by minor improvements, not major alterations (Hollander, 1965). The point is that the incremental approach used in a small-wins strategy is the most basic and the one most compatible with human preferences for learning, perception, motivation and change (Weick, 1984).

What does this have to do with hardiness and resilience? A small-wins strategy both engenders hardiness and helps overcome the Type A personality syndrome, which is basically a large-win, winner-takes-all approach to stress. You may recall that hardiness is composed of control, commitment and challenge. The deliberate cultivation of a strategy of small wins helps produce precisely those psychological states. Small wins reinforce the perception that individuals can influence what happens to them (being in control); it helps motivate further action by building on the confidence of past successes (which creates commitment); and it produces changes of manageable size that serve as incentives to broaden, learn and seek new opportunities (or challenges). 'Continuing pursuit of small wins can build increasing resistance to stress in people not originally predisposed toward hardiness' (Weick, 1984, p. 46).

Deep-Relaxation Strategies

In addition to a small-wins strategy, a second approach to building psychological resilience is to learn and practice a deep-relaxation technique. Research demonstrates a marked decrease in Type A personality characteristics for regular users of meditation and deep relaxation techniques. Using the car analogy, individuals who use deep-relaxation exercises find that when stress occurs their 'engines' don't rev up as high and they return to idle faster (Curtis and Detert, 1981; Greenberg, 1987; Davis, McKay and Eshelman,

1980). Deep-relaxation techniques differ from temporary, short-term relaxation techniques, which we will discuss later. Deep relaxation, like physical exercise, takes time to develop because its benefits cannot be achieved quickly, but it serves to engender resilience toward stress.

Deep-relaxation techniques include meditation, yoga, autogenic training or self-hypnosis, biofeedback, and so on. Considerable evidence exists that individuals who practice such techniques regularly are able to condition their bodies to inhibit the negative effects of stress (Cooper and Aygen, 1979; Stone and Deleo, 1976; Orme-Johnson, 1973; Beary and Benson, 1977; Benson, 1975). Most of these deep-relaxation techniques must be practised over a period of time in order to develop fully, but they are not difficult to learn. Most deep-relaxation techniques require the following conditions:

1. A quiet environment in which external distractions are minimised.
2. A comfortable position so that musular effort is minimised.
3. A mental focus. Transcendental meditation (TM) advocates recommend concentrating on one word, phrase or object. Benson (1975) suggests the word 'one'. Others suggest picturing a plain vase. The ancient Chinese used a carved jade object that resembled a mountain, sitting on a desk-top. The purpose of focusing on a word or object is to rid the mind of all other thoughts.
4. Controlled breathing, i.e., deliberate breathing, with pauses between breaths. Thoughts are focused on rhythmic breathing, which helps clear the mind and aids concentration.
5. A passive attitude, so that if other thoughts enter the mind they are ignored.
6. Focused bodily changes. While meditation uses the mind to relax the body, autogenic training used bodily sensations of heaviness and warmth to change the psychological state. Feelings of warmth and heaviness are induced in different parts of the body which, in turn, create deep relaxation (Luthe, 1962; Kamiya, 1978).

7. Repetition. Because physiological and psychological results depend on consistent practice, the best results occur when such techniques are practised from 20 to 30 minutes each day.

The Skill Practice section (page 82) contains an example of a deep relaxation exercise.

Social Resilience

The third factor moderating the harmful effects of stress and contributing to resilience involves developing close social relationships. Individuals who are embedded in supportive social networks are less likely to experience stress and are better equipped to cope with its consequences (Beehr, 1976). Supportive social relations provide opportunities to share one's frustrations and disappointments, to receive suggestions and encouragement, and to experience emotional bonding. Such supportive interactions provide the empathy and bolstering required to cope with stressful events. They are formed most easily among individuals who share close emotional ties (e.g., family members) or common experiences (e.g., co-workers).

Dramatic evidence for the value of social support systems during periods of high stress comes from the experiences of soldiers captured during World War II and the Korean and Vietnam wars. When it was possible for prisoners to form permanent, interacting groups, they maintained better health and morale and were able to resist their captors more effectively than when they were isolated or when groups were unstable. Indeed, the well-documented technique used by the Chinese during the Korean War for breaking down soldiers' resistance to their indoctrination efforts involved weakening group solidarity through planting seeds of mistrust and doubt about members' loyalty.

Apart from personal friendships or family relations, two types of social support systems can be formed as part of a manager's job. One is a mentor relationship; the other is a task team. Most individuals, with the possible exception of the most senior managers, can profit from a mentoring relationship. The research is clear, in fact, that career success, work satisfaction and resilience to stress are enhanced by a mentoring relationship (Hall, 1976; Kram, 1985). Individuals need someone else in the organisation who can provide a role model, from whom they can learn, and from whom they can receive personal attention and a reinforcement of self-worth, especially under uncertain, crucial and stressful situations.

Many organisations formally prescribe a mentoring system by assigning a senior manager to shepherd a younger manager when he or she enters the organisation. With rare exceptions, when the contact is one-way, from the top down, these relationships don't work out (Kram, 1985). The junior manager must actively seek and foster the mentoring relationship as well. The junior manager can do this, not by demonstrating over-dependence or over adaptation, but by expressing a desire to use the senior person as a mentor and then by making certain that the relationship does not become a one-way street. The subordinate can pass along important information and resources to the potential mentor, while both will share in working out solutions to problems. That way, the mentoring relationship becomes mutually satisfying and beneficial for both parties, and resilience to stress is enhanced because of the commitment, trust and co-operation that begin to characterise the relationship. A mentor's guidance can both help avoid stressful situations and provide support for coping with them.

Smoothly functioning work teams also enhance social resilience. The social value of working on a team has been well-documented in research (Dyer, 1981). The more cohesive the team, the more support it provides its members. Members of highly cohesive teams communicate with one another more frequently and positively, and report higher satisfaction, lower stress and higher performance levels than do individuals who do not feel as though they are part of a work team (Shaw, 1976).

The value of work teams has been amply demonstrated in practice as well. For example, in the Fremont, California plant of General Motors a dramatic change occurred when U.S. workers came under Japanese management. In just one year, marked improvements in productivity, morale and quality occurred, due in large part to the use of effective work teams. Relationships were formed based not only on friendship, but on a common commitment to solving work-related problems and to generating ideas for improvement. Teams met regularly during work hours to discuss ideas for improvement and to co-ordinate and resolve issues.

Similar dynamics have been fostered in many of the successful companies in Europe. Changes at British Aerospace have been attributed largely to the effective use of work teams. The marked improvements that occur in individual satisfaction and lowered stress levels suggest that each person should likewise help facilitate similar teamwork in his or her work setting as part of a social resilience repertoire. To do so, individuals might consider identifying and structuring team tasks or team issues; facilitating a culture of continuous improvement among co-workers where everyone takes responsibility for generating and sharing ideas for improvement; and sharing information or resources in such a way that the team, rather than independent individuals, becomes the basic unit of action.

Temporary Stress-Reduction Techniques

Thus, so far we have emphasised eliminating sources of stress and developing resilience to stress. These are the most desirable stress-management strategies. However, even under ideal circumstances it may be impossible to eliminate all stressors, and individuals must use temporary reactive mechanisms in order to maintain equilibrium. Although increased resilience can buffer the harmful effects of stress, people must sometimes take immediate action in the short term to cope with stress. Implementing short-term strategies reduces stress temporarily so that longer-term stress-elimination or resilience strategies can operate. Short-term strategies are largely reactive and must be repeated whenever stressors are encountered because, unlike other strategies, their effects are only temporary. On the other hand, they are especially useful for immediately calming feelings of anxiety or apprehension. Individuals can use them when they are asked a question they can't answer, when they become embarrassed by an unexpected event, when they are faced with a presentation or an important meeting, or almost any time they are suddenly stressed and must respond in a short period of time. Five of the best-known and easiest to learn techniques are briefly described below. The first two are physiological; the last three are psychological.

Muscle Relaxation

Muscle relaxation involves easing the tension in successive muscle groups. Each muscle group is tightened for five or ten seconds, then completely relaxed. Starting with the feet and progressing to the calves, thighs, stomach, and on to the neck and face, one can relieve tension throughout the entire body. All parts of the body can be included in the exercise. One variation is to roll the head around on the neck several times, shrug the shoulders or stretch the arms up toward the ceiling for five to ten seconds, then release the position and relax the muscles. The result is a state of temporary relaxation that helps eliminate tension and refocus energy.

The Management Training Centre of Unilever UK Holdings in Port Sunlight, UK, was well know for promoting a particular technique of relaxation at meetings. Individuals, feeling under stress, were encouraged to push hard on the underside of the table with their little fingers. The legend was that after several years and several generations of managers had been training in this technique, the table spontaneously levitated at Unilever Board meeting. After this incident, training in the technique was stopped.

Deep Breathing

A variation of muscle relaxation involves deep breathing. This is done by taking several successive, slow, deep breaths, holding them for five seconds and exhaling completely. You should focus on breathing itself, so that the mind becomes cleared for a brief time while the body relaxes. After each deep breath, muscles in the body should consciously be relaxed.

Imagery and Fantasy

A third technique uses imagery and fantasy to eliminate stress temporarily by changing the focus of one's thoughts. Imagery involves visualising an event, using 'mind pictures.' In addition to visualisation, however, imagery also can include recollections of sounds, smells and textures. The mind focuses on pleasant experiences from the past (e.g., a fishing trip, family holiday, visit with relatives, a day at the beach) that can be recalled vividly. Fantasies, on the other hand, are not past memories but make-believe events or images. It is especially well-known, for example, that children often construct imaginary friends, make-believe occurrences or special wishes that are comforting to them when they encounter stress. Adults also use daydreams or other fantasy experiences to get them through stressful situations. The purpose of this technique is to relieve anxiety or pressure temporarily by focusing on something pleasant so that other more productive stress-reducing strategies can be developed for the longer term.

Rehearsal

The fourth technique is called rehearsal. Using this technique, people work themselves through potentially stressful situations, trying out different scenarios and alternative reactions. Appropriate reactions are rehearsed, either in a safe environment before stress occurs, or 'off-line', in private, in the midst of a stressful situation. Removing oneself temporarily from a stressful circumstance and working through dialogue or reactions, as though rehearsing for a play, can help an individual regain control and reduce the immediacy of the stressor.

Reframing

The last strategy, reframing, involves temporarily reducing stress by optimistically redefining a situation as manageable. Although reframing is difficult in the midst of a stressful situation, it can be facilitated by using the following cues:

> 'I understand this situation.'
> 'I've solved similar problems before.'
> 'Other people are available to help me get through this situation.'
> 'Others have faced similar situations and made it through.'
> 'In the long run, this really isn't so critical.'
> 'I can learn something from this situation.'
> 'There are several good alternatives available to me.'

Each of these statements can assist an individual to reframe a situation in order to develop long-term proactive or enactive strategies.

Summary

We began this book by explaining stress in terms of a relatively simple model. Four kinds of stressors – time, encounter, situational and anticipatory – cause negative physiological, psychological and social reactions in individuals. These reactions are moderated by the resilience that individuals have developed for coping with stress. The best way to manage stress is to eliminate it through time management, delegation, collaboration, interpersonal competence, work redesign, prioritising, goal setting and small wins.

The next most effective stress management strategy is improving one's resilience. Physiological resilience is strengthened through increased cardiovascular conditioning and improved diet. Psychological resilience and hardiness is improved by practising small-wins strategies and deep relaxation. Social resilience is increased by fostering mentoring relationships and teamwork among colleagues.

However, when circumstances make it impossible to apply longer-term strategies for reducing stress, short-term relaxation techniques can temporarily alleviate the symptoms of stress.

Behavioural Guidelines

The following are specific behavioural guidelines for improving one's stress management skills.

1. Use effective time management practices. Make sure that you use time effectively as well as efficiently by generating your own personal mission statement. Make sure that low-priority tasks do not drive out time to work on high-priority activities. Make better use of your time by using the guidelines in the Time Management Survey (page 5).
2. Build collaborative relationships with individuals based on mutual trust, respect, honesty and kindness. Make 'deposits' into the 'emotional bank accounts' of other people. Form close, stable communities among those with whom you work.
3. Consciously work to improve your interpersonal competency.
4. Redesign your work to increase its skill variety, importance, task identity (comprehensiveness), autonomy and feedback. Make the work itself stress-reducing, rather than stress-inducing.
5. Reaffirm priorities and short-term plans that provide direction and focus to activities. Give important activities priority over urgent ones.

6. Increase your general resilience by leading a balanced life and consciously developing yourself in physical, intellectual, cultural, social, family and spiritual areas, as well as in your work.
7. Increase your physical resilience by engaging in a regular programme of exercise and proper eating.
8. Increase your psychological resilience and hardiness by implementing a small wins strategy. Identify and celebrate the small successes that you and others achieve.
9. Learn at least one deep-relaxation technique and practice it regularly.
10. Increase social resilience by forming an open, trusting, sharing relationship with at least one other person. Facilitate a mentoring relationship with someone who can affirm your worth as a person and provide support during periods of stress.
11. Establish a teamwork relationship with those with whom you work or study by identifying shared tasks and structuring co-ordinated action among team members.
12. Learn at least two short-term relaxation techniques and practice them consistently.

Skill Analysis

Cases Involving Stress Management

The Day at the Beach

Not long ago I came to one of those bleak periods that many of us encounter from time to time, a sudden drastic dip in the graph of living when everything goes stale and flat, energy wanes, enthusiasm dies. The effect on my work was frightening. Every morning I would clench my teeth and mutter: 'Today life will take on some of its old meaning. You've got to break through this thing. You've got to!'

But the barren days went by, and the paralysis grew worse. The time came when I knew I had to have help. The man I turned to was a doctor. Not a psychiatrist, just a doctor. He was older than I, and under his surface gruffness lay great wisdom and compassion. 'I don't know what's wrong,' I told him miserably, 'but I just seem to have come to a dead end. Can you help me?'

'I don't know,' he said slowly. He made a tent of his fingers and gazed at me thoughtfully for a long while. Then, abruptly, he asked, 'Where were you happiest as a child?'

'As a child?' I echoed. 'Why, at the beach, I suppose. We had a summer cottage there. We all loved it.'

He looked out the window and watched the October leaves sifting down.

'Are you capable of following instructions for a single day?'

'I think so,' I said, ready to try anything.

'All right. Here's what I want you to do.'

I was living in The Hague at the time and he told me to drive down to a quieter part of the local beach by myself the following morning, arriving not later than nine o'clock. I could take some lunch, but I was not to read, write, listen to the radio or talk to anyone. 'In addition,' he said, 'I'll give you a prescription to be taken every three hours.'

He tore off four prescription blanks, wrote a few words on each, folded them, numbered them and handed them to me.

'Take these at nine, twelve, three, and six.'

'Are you serious?' I asked.

He gave a short bark of laughter.

'You won't think I'm joking when you get my bill!'

The next morning, with little faith, I drove to the beach. It was lonely, all right. A northeaster was blowing; the sea looked grey and angry. I sat in the car, the whole day stretching emptily before me. Then I took out the first of the folded slips of paper. On it was written: LISTEN CAREFULLY.

I stared at the two words. 'Why,' I thought, 'the man must be mad.' He had ruled out music, newscasts and human conversation. What else was there?

I raised my head and I did listen. There were no sounds but the steady roar of the sea, the creaking cry of a gull, the drone of some aircraft high overhead. All these sounds were familiar.

I got out of the car. A gust of wind slammed the door with a sudden clap of sound. 'Was I supposed to listen carefully to things like that?' I asked myself.

I looked out over the deserted beach, it was winter and not a very nice day. Here the sea bellowed so loudly that all other sounds were lost. And yet, I thought suddenly, there must be sounds beneath sounds – the soft rasp of drifting sand, the tiny wind-whisperings in the dune grasses – if the listener got close enough to hear them.

On an impulse I ducked down and, feeling fairly ridiculous, thrust my head into a clump of seaweed. Here I made a discovery: if you listen intently, there is a fractional moment in which everything seems to pause. In that instant of stillness, the racing thoughts halt. For a moment, when you truly listen for something outside yourself, you have to silence the clamorous voices within. The mind rests.

I went back to the car and slid behind the wheel. LISTEN CAREFULLY. As I listened again to the deep growl of the sea, I found myself thinking about the white-fanged fury of its storms. I thought of the lessons it had taught us as children. A certain amount of patience: you can't hurry the tides. A great deal of respect: the sea does not suffer fools gladly. An awareness of the vast and mysterious interdependence of things: wind, and tide and current, calm and squall and hurricane, all combining to determine the paths of the birds above and the fish below. And the cleanliness of it all, with every beach swept twice a day by the great broom of the sea.

Sitting there, I realised I was thinking of things bigger than myself – and there was relief in that.

Even so, the morning passed slowly. The habit of hurling myself at a problem was so strong that I felt lost without it. Once, when I was wistfully eyeing the car radio, a phrase from Carlyle jumped into my head: 'Silence is the element in which great things fashion themselves.'

By noon the wind had polished the clouds out of the sky, and the sea had a hard, polished and merry sparkle. I unfolded the second 'prescription'. Again I sat there, half-amused and half-exasperated. Three words this time: TRY REACHING BACK.

Back to what? To the past, obviously. But why, when all my worries concerned the present or the future?

I left the car and started tramping back. The doctor had sent me to the beach because it was a place of happy memories. Maybe that was what I was supposed to reach for: the wealth of happiness that lay half-forgotten behind me.

I decided to experiment: to work on these vague impressions as a painter would, retouching the colours, strengthening the outlines. I would choose specific incidents and recapture as many details as possible. I would visualise people complete with dress and gestures. I would listen (carefully) for the exact sound of their voices, the echo of their laughter.

The tide was going out now, but there was still thunder in the surf. So I chose to go back twenty years to the last fishing trip I made with my younger brother. (He died in the Battle of the Atlantic World War II and his body was never recovered.) I found that if I closed my eyes and really tried, I could see him with amazing vividness, even the humour and eagerness in his eyes that far-off morning.

In fact, I could see it all: the ivory scimitar of beach where we were fishing; the sky smeared with sunrise; the great rollers creaming in, stately and slow. I could feel the backwash swirl warm around my knees, see the sudden arc of my brother's rod as he struck a fish, hear his exultant yell. Piece by piece I rebuilt it, clear and unchanged under the transparent varnish of time. Then it was gone.

I sat up slowly. TRY REACHING BACK. Happy people were usually assured, confident people. If, then, you deliberately reached back and touched happiness, might there not be released little flashes of power, tiny sources of strength?

This second period of the day went more quickly, people appeared and seemed themselves to resent each other, keeping in little knots of privacy. As the sun began its long slant down the sky, my mind ranged eagerly through the past, reliving some episodes, uncovering others that had been completely forgotten. For example, when I was around thirteen and my brother ten, Father had promised to take us to the circus. But at lunch there was a phone call: some urgent business required his attention. We braced ourselves for disappointment. Then we heard him say, 'No, I won't be down. It'll have to wait.' When he came back to the table, Mother smiled. 'The circus keeps coming back, you know.'

'I know,' said Father. 'But childhood doesn't.'

Across all the years I remembered this and knew from the sudden glow of warmth that no kindness is ever wasted or ever completely lost. By three o'clock the tide was out and the sound of the waves was only a rhythmic whisper, like a giant breathing. I stayed in my sandy nest, feeling relaxed and content, and a little complacent. The doctor's prescriptions, I thought, were easy to take.

But I was not prepared for the next one. This time the three words were not a gentle suggestion. They sounded more like a command. RE-EXAMINE YOUR MOTIVES. My first reaction was purely defensive. 'There's nothing wrong with my motives,' I said to myself. 'I want to be successful – who doesn't? I want to have a certain amount of recognition – but so does everybody. I want more security than I've got – and why not?'

'Maybe,' said a small voice somewhere inside my head, 'those motives aren't good enough. Maybe that's the reason the wheels have stopped going around.'

I picked up a handful of sand and let it stream between my fingers. In the past, whenever my work went well, there had always been something spontaneous about it, something uncontrived, something free. Lately it had been calculated, competent and dead. Why? Because I had been looking past the job itself to the rewards I hoped it would bring. The work had ceased to be an end in itself, it had been merely a means to make money, pay bills. The sense of giving something, of helping people, of making a contribution, had been lost in a frantic clutch at security.

In a flash of certainty, I saw that if one's motives are wrong, nothing can be right. It makes no difference whether you are a postman, a hairdresser, an insurance salesman, a housewife . . . As long as you feel you are serving others, you do the job well. When you are concerned only with helping yourself, you do it less well. There is a law as inexorable as gravity.

For a long time I sat there. Far out on the bar I heard the murmur of the surf change to a hollow roar as the tide turned. Behind me the spears of light were almost horizontal. My time at the beach had almost run out, and I felt a grudging admiration for the doctor and the 'prescriptions' he had so casually and cunningly devised. I saw, now, that in them was a therapeutic progression that might well be of value to anyone facing any difficulty.

LISTEN CAREFULLY: To calm a frantic mind, slow it down, shift the focus from inner problems to outer things.

TRY REACHING BACK: Since the human mind can hold but one idea at a time, you blot out present worry when you touch the happiness of the past.

RE-EXAMINE YOUR MOTIVES: This was the hard core of the 'treatment', this challenge to reappraise, to bring one's motives into alignment with one's capabilities and conscience. But the mind must be clear and receptive to do this – hence the six hours of quiet that went before.

The western sky was a blaze of crimson as I took out the last slip of paper. Six words this time. I walked slowly out on the beach. A few yards below the high water mark I stopped and read the words again: WRITE YOUR TROUBLES ON THE SAND.

I let the paper blow away, reached down and picked up a fragment of shell. Kneeling there under the vault of the sky, I wrote several words on the sand, one above the other. Then I walked away, and I did not look back. I had written my troubles on the sand. And the tide was coming in.

(Source: adapted from *The Day at the Beach*, by Arthur Gordon. Copyright 1959, by Arthur Gordon. First published in *Reader's Digest*. Reprinted by permission of the author. All rights reserved.)

Discussion Questions

1. What is effective about these strategies for coping with stress? Why did they work? Upon what principles are they based?
2. Which of these techniques can be used on a temporary basic without going to the beach?
3. Are these prescriptions effective coping strategies or merely escapes?
4. What other prescriptions could the author take besides the four mentioned here? Generate your own list.
5. What do these prescriptions have to do with the model of stress management presented in this book?

The Case of the Missing Time

At approximately 7.30 a.m. on Tuesday, June 23, 1989, Chris Craig, a senior production manager in the Norris Printing Ltd, set off to drive to work. It was a beautiful day and the journey to the factory took about 20 minutes giving Chris an opportunity to think about plant problems without interruption.

The Norris Company owned and operated three factories and had a Europe-wide reputation for quality colour printing. Three hundred and fifty people worked for the company, about half working in Chris's Belgium plant which also housed the company's head quarters

Chris was in fine spirits as he relaxed behind the wheel. Various thoughts occurred to him, and he said to himself, 'This is going to be the day to really get things done.'

He began to run through the day's work, first one project, then another, trying to establish priorities. After a few minutes he decided that progressing the new system of production control was probably the most important, certainly the most urgent of his jobs for the day. He frowned for a moment as he remembered that on Friday the general manager had casually asked him if he had given the project any further thought. Chris realised that he had not been giving it much thought lately. He had been meaning to get to work on this idea for over three months, but something else always seemed to crop up. 'I haven't had much time to sit down and really work it out,' he said to himself. 'I'd better get going and sort this one out today.' With that, he began to break down the objectives, procedures, and installation steps of the project. He grinned as he reviewed the principles involved and calculated roughly the anticipated savings. 'It's about time,' he told himself. 'This idea should have been followed up long ago.' Chris remembered that he had first thought of the production control system nearly eighteen months ago, just prior to his leaving Norris's factory in Spain. He had spoken to his boss, Jim Quince, manager of the Spanish factory about it then, and both agreed that it was worth looking into. The idea was temporarily shelved when he was transferred to the Belgium plant a month later.

Then he started to think through a procedure for simpler transport of dyes to and from the Spanish plant. Visualising the notes on his desk, he thought about the inventory analysis he needed to identify and eliminate some of the slow-moving stock items, the packing controls that needed revision and the need to design a new special-order form. He also decided that this was the day to settle on a job printer to do the simple outside printing of office forms. There were a few other projects he couldn't remember, but he could tend to them after lunch, if not before.

But when he entered the plant Chris knew something was wrong as he met Albert Marsden, the stockroom foreman, who appeared troubled.

'A great morning, Albert,' Chris greeted him cheerfully.

'Not so good, Chris; the new man isn't in this morning.'

'Did he phone in – let you known why?' asked Chris.

'No, nothing,' replied Marsden.

Chris shared Albert's concern, he knew that 'the new man' had been taken on to cover for a major problem in the warehouse. Without him, and in particularly without him at no notice, the whole of the new automated stock delivery system could and probably would grind to a halt.

'OK, we have problem. Ask personnel to call him and see if he intends to come in.'

Albert Marsden hesitated for a moment before replying, 'Okay, Chris, but can you find me a man with some sort of computer skills – you know the problem as well as I do.'

'OK, Albert, I'll call you in half an hour with something, even if I have to do it myself.'

Making a mental note of the situation, Chris headed for his office. He greeted the group of workers huddled around Marie, the office manager, who was discussing the day's work schedule with them. As the meeting broke up, Marie picked up a few samples from the pallet, showed them to Chris, and asked if they should be sent out as they were or whether it would be necessary to inspect all of them. Before he could answer, Marie went on to ask if he could suggest another operator for the sealing machine to replace the regular operator, who was absent. She also told him that George, the industrial engineer, had called and was waiting to hear from Chris.

After telling Marie to send the samples as they were, he made a note of the need for a sealer operator for the office and then called George. He agreed to go to George's office before lunch and started on his routine morning tour of the factory. He asked each foreman the types and volumes of orders they were running, the number of people present, how the schedules were coming along, and the orders to be run next. He helped the folding-room foreman find temporary storage space for consolidating a consignment; discussed quality control with a press operator who had been producing work off specification; arranged to transfer four people temporarily to different departments, including one for Albert from accounts who 'was not frightened of computers'; and talked to the shipping foreman about collecting some urgent ink supplies and the special deliveries of the day. As he continued through the factory, he saw to it that reserve stock was moved out of the forward stock area; talked to another pressman about his holiday; had a 'heart-to-heart' talk with a press assistant who seemed to need frequent reassurance; and approved two-type and one colour-changes with three press operators and their team leader.

Returning to his office, Chris reviewed the production reports on the larger orders against his initial estimates and found that the plant was running behind schedule. He called in the folding-room team leader and together they went over production schedule in detail, making several changes.

During this discussion, the composing-room foreman stopped in to note several type changes, and the routing foreman telephoned for approval of a revised printing schedule. The stockroom foreman called twice, first to inform him that two standard, fast-moving stock items were dangerously low, and later to advise him that the paper stock for the urgent Harper Collins job had finally arrived. Chris made the necessary subsequent calls to inform those concerned.

He then began to put delivery dates on important and difficult inquiries received from customers and salesmen. (The routine inquiries were handled by Marie.) While he was doing this he was interrupted twice, once by a sales rep to ask for a better delivery date than originally scheduled, and once by the personnel director asking him to set a time when he could hold an initial training and induction interview with a new employee.

After sorting the customer and salesmen inquiries, Chris headed for his morning conference in the executive offices. At this meeting he answered the sales director's questions in connection with some problem orders, complaints, and the status of large-volume orders and potential new orders. He then met the general manager to discuss a few ticklish policy matters and to answer 'the old man's' questions on several specific production and personnel problems. Before leaving the executive offices, he stopped at the office of the secretary-treasurer to inquire about delivery of cartons, paper and boxes, and to place a new order for paper.

On the way back to his own office, Chris conferred with George about the current engineering projects which he had called about earlier. When he reached his desk, he looked at his watch. He had five minute before lunch – enough to make a few notes of the details he needed to check in order to answer knotty questions raised by the sales manager that morning.

After lunch Chris started again. He began by checking the previous day's production reports, did some rescheduling to get out urgent orders, placed appropriate delivery dates on new orders and inquiries received that morning, and consulted with a foreman on a personal problem. He spent about twenty minutes on the phone going over mutual problems with the Spanish factory.

By mid afternoon Chris had made another tour of the site, after which he met with the personnel director to review a touchy personal problem raised by one of the clerical employees; the holiday schedules submitted by his foremen; and the pending job-evaluation programme. Following this conference, Chris hurried back to his office to complete the special statistical report for U.W.C., one of Norris's best customers. As he finished the report, he discovered that it was ten minutes past six and he was the only one left in the office. Chris was tired. He put on his coat and headed for his car; on the way he was stopped by both the night supervisor and night layout foremen for approval of type and layout changes.

With both eyes on the traffic, Chris reviewed the day he had just completed. 'Busy?' he asked himself. 'Too busy – but did I actually DO anything? There was the usual routine, the same as any other day. The factory kept going and I think it must have been a good production day. Any creative or special project work done?' Chris grimaced as he reluctantly answered, 'No.'

Feeling guilty, he probed further. 'Am I a senior manager – a true executive? I'm paid like one, respected like one, and have a responsible assignment with the necessary authority to carry it out. Yet an executive should be able to think strategically and creatively, not just fire-fight. An executive needs time for thinking. Today was typical and I did little, if any, creative work. The projects that I planned in the morning have not moved an inch. What's more, I have no guarantee that tomorrow or the next day will be any different. This is the real problem.'

Chris continued, 'Taking work home? Yes, occasionally, its expected but I've been doing too much lately. I owe my wife and family some of my time. When you come down to it, they are the people for whom I'm really working. If I am forced to spend much more time away from them, am I being fair to them or myself. What about work with the

Scouts? Should I stop it? It takes up a lot of my time, but I feel I owe other people some time, and I feel that I am making a valuable contribution. When do I have time for a game of squash or even a quiet drink with my friends these days?'

Chris worried. 'Maybe I'm just making excuses because I don't plan my time better, but I don't think so. I've already analysed my way of working and I think I plan and delegate pretty well. Do I need an assistant? Possibly, but that's a long-term project and I don't believe I could justify the additional overhead expenditure. Anyway, I doubt whether it would solve the problem.'

All the way home he was concerned with the problem – even as he pulled into the drive. His thoughts were interrupted as he saw his son running towards the car – 'Mummy, Daddy's home.'

Discussion Questions

1. Which of Chris's personal characteristics inhibit his effective management of time?
2. What are his organisational problems?
3. What principles of time and stress management are violated in this case?
4. If you were hired as a consultant to Chris, what would you advise him to do?

Skill Practice

Exercises for Long- and Short-Term Stress Management

In this section we provide four relatively short exercises to help you practice good stress management. We strongly urge you to complete the exercises with a partner who can give you feedback on how you do, and who will monitor your progress in improving your skill. Because managing stress is a personal skill, most of your practice will be done in private. But having a partner who is aware of your commitment will help foster substantial improvement.

The Small-Wins Strategy

Background
An ancient Chinese proverb states that long journeys are always made up of small steps. In Japan, the feeling of obligation to make small, incremental improvements in one's work is known as 'Kaizen'. In this book the notion of small wins was explained as a way to break apart large problems and identify small successes in coping with them. Each of these approaches represents the same basic philosophy – to recognise incremental successes – and each helps an individual build up psychological resilience to stress.

Assignment
Answer the following questions. An example is given to help clarify each question, but your response need not relate to the example.

1. What major stressor do you currently face? What creates anxiety or discomfort for you? (For example, 'I have too much to do.')
2. What are the major attributes or components of the situation? Divide the major problem into smaller parts or sub-problems. (For example, 'I have said *yes* to too many things. I have deadlines

approaching. I don't have all the resources I need to complete all my commitments right now.')
3. What are the sub-components of each of those sub-problems? Divide them into yet smaller parts. (For example, 'I have the following deadlines approaching: a report due, a large amount of reading to do, a family obligation, an important presentation, a need to spend some personal time with someone I care about, and a committee meeting that requires preparation.')
4. What actions can I take that will affect any of these sub-components? (For example, 'I can engage the person I care about in helping me prepare for the presentation. I can write a shorter report than I originally intended. I can carry the reading material with me wherever I go.')
5. What actions have I taken in the past that have helped me cope successfully with similar stressful circumstances? (For example, 'I have found someone else to share some of my tasks. I have got some reading done while waiting, riding and eating. I have prepared only key elements for the committee meeting.')
6. What small thing should I feel good about as I think about how I have coped or will cope with this major stressor? (For example, 'I have accomplished a lot when the pressure has been on in the past. I have been able to use what I had time to prepare to its best advantage.')

Repeat this process every time you face major stressors. The six specific questions may not be as important to you as:

- Breaking the problem down into incremental parts and then breaking those parts down again
- Identifying alternative actions that can be done and have been done in the past, and that have been successful in coping with components of the stressor.

Life-Balance Analysis

Background
The prescription to maintain a balanced life seems to contain a paradox:

- It makes sense that life should have variety and that each of us should develop multiple aspects of ourselves. Narrowness and rigidity are not highly valued by anyone.

■ However the demands of work, school or family, for example, can be so overwhelming that we don't have time to do much except respond to those demands. Work could take all of one's time. So could school. So could family. The temptation for most of us, then, is to focus on only a few areas of our lives that place a great deal of pressure on us, leaving the other areas undeveloped.

This exercise helps you discover which areas those might be and which areas you need to give more attention.

Assignment
Use Figure 5 (page 50) to complete this exercise. In responding to the four items in the exercise, think of the amount of time you spend in each area; the amount of experience and development you have had in the past in each area; and the extent to which development in each area is important to you.

1. In Figure 5, shade in the portion of each section that represents the extent to which that aspect of your life has been well developed. How satisfied are you that each aspect is adequately cultivated?
2. Now write down at least one thing you can start doing to improve your development in the areas that need it. For example, you might do more outside reading to develop culturally; invite a foreign visitor to your home to develop socially; engage in regular prayer to develop spiritually; and so on.
3. Because the intent of this exercise is not to add more pressure and stress to your life, but to increase your resilience through life balance, identify the things you will stop doing that will make it possible to achieve a better life balance.
4. To make this a practice exercise and not just a planning exercise, do something today that you have on your list for items two and three above. Write down specifically what you'll do and when. Don't let the rest of the week go by without implementing something you've written.

Deep Relaxation

Background

To engage in deep relaxation, you need to reserve time that can be spent concentrating on relaxing. Cognitive control and physiological control are involved. By focusing your mind, you can positively affect both your mental and physical states. This exercise describes one technique that is easily learned and practised.

Assignment

The deep-relaxation technique presented below combines key elements of several well-known formulas. It is recommended that this technique be practised for 20 minutes a day, three times a week (Davis, Eshelman, and McKay, 1980). Reserve at least 30 minutes to engage in this exercise for the first time. Find a quiet spot with your partner and have that person read the instructions below. When you have finished, switch roles. Since you will practice this exercise later in a different setting, you may want to make a tape recording of these instructions, or do the exercise with a friend or a spouse.

Step 1: Assume a comfortable position. You may want to lie down. Loosen any tight clothing. Close your eyes and be quiet.

Step 2: Assume a passive attitude. Focus on your body and on relaxing specific muscles. Tune out all other thoughts.

Step 3: Tense and relax each of your muscle groups for five to ten seconds, in the following order:

Forehead – Wrinkle your forehead. Try to make your eyebrows touch your hairline for five seconds, then relax.

Eyes and nose – Close your eyes as tightly as you can for five seconds, then relax.

Lips, cheeks and jaw – Draw the corners of your mouth back and grimace for five seconds and then relax.

Hands – Extend your arms in front of you. Clench your fists tightly for five seconds, then relax.

Forearms – Extend your arms out against an invisible wall and push forward for five seconds, then relax.

Upper arms – Bend your elbows and tense your biceps for five seconds, then relax.

Shoulders – Shrug your shoulders up to your ears for five seconds, then relax.

Back – Arch your back off the floor for five seconds, then relax.

Stomach – Tighten your stomach muscles by lifting your legs off the ground about two inches for five seconds, then relax.

Hips and buttocks – Tighten your hip and buttock muscles for five seconds, then relax.

Thighs – Tighten your thigh muscles by pressing your legs together as tightly as you can for five seconds, then relax.

Feet – Bend your ankles toward your body as far as you can for five seconds, then point your toes for five seconds, then relax.

Toes – Curl your toes as tightly as you can for five seconds, then relax.

Step 4: Focus on any muscles that are still tense. Repeat the exercise for that muscle group three or four times until it relaxes.

Step 5: Now focus on your breathing. Do not alter it artificially, but focus on taking long, slow breaths. Concentrate exclusively on the rhythm of your breathing until you have taken at least 45 breaths.

Step 6: Now focus on the heaviness and warmth of your body. Let all the energy in your body seep away. Let go of your normal tendency to control your body and mobilise it toward activity.

Step 7: With your body completely relaxed, relax your mind. Picture a plain object such as a glass ball, an empty white vase, the moon or some favourite thing. Don't analyse it; don't examine it; just picture it. Concentrate fully on the object for at least three minutes without letting any other thoughts enter your mind. Begin now.

Step 8: Now open your eyes, slowly get up, and return to your hectic, stressful, anxiety-ridden, Type A environment better prepared to cope with it effectively.

Monitoring and Managing Time

Background

Managers and business school students very often identify time management as their most pressing problem. They feel overwhelmed at times with the feeling of not having achieved those things that they know they could have achieved. However, even though people may be extremely busy, they experience less dysfunctional stress if they feel they are in control of their time, and in particular, able to take time out. It is the existence of time that is under your control, which includes time out – discretionary time, that is a key to effective time management. This exercise helps you identify and better manage your discretionary time.

Assignment

This exercise in some form is a key element in most time management programmes. It takes one week to complete and requires you to keep a time diary for the whole period.

Complete the following five steps, then use your partner to get feedback and ideas for improving and refining your plans.

Step 1: Beginning tomorrow, keep a time diary for a whole week. Record how you spend each thirty-minute block in the next seven 24 hour periods. Using the following format in a suitable notebook you can carry with you.

Time	Required/ Discretionary	Activity	Productive/ Unproductive
1:00-1:30			
1:30-2:00			
2:00-2:30			

.

Step 2: Beneath the heading 'Required/Discretionary', write whether the time spent in each 30-minute block was required by someone or something else (R), or was discretionary (D).

Step 3: Beneath the heading 'Productive/Unproductive', and beside only the discretionary time blocks, rate the extent to which you used each one productively, that is, whether or not it led to improvements of some kind. Use the following scale for your rating:

    4 – Used productively
    3 – Used somewhat productively
    2 – Used somewhat unproductively
    1 – Used unproductively

Step 4: Draw up a plan for increasing the amount of discretionary time you have during the week. The hints in the Time Management Survey on page 00 can provide some suggestions. Write down below the things you will implement.

Step 5: Identify ways in which you can use your discretionary time more productively, especially any blocks of time you rated one or two in step three. What will you do to make sure the time you control is used for more long-term benefit? What will you stop doing that impedes your effective use of time?

Skill Application

Application Activities For Managing Stress

Suggested Further Assignments

1. Do a systematic analysis of the stressors you face in your job, family, college and social life. List the types of stressors you face, and identify strategies to eliminate or sharply reduce them. Record this analysis in your journal.

2. Find someone you know well who is experiencing a great deal of stress. Teach him or her how to manage that stress better by applying the concepts, principles, techniques, and exercises in this book. Describe what you taught and record the results in your journal.

3. Implement at least three of the time-management techniques suggested in the Time Management Survey, or elsewhere, that you are not currently using but think you might find helpful. In your time diary, keep track of the amount of time these techniques save you over a one-month period. Be sure to use that extra time productively.

4. With a co-worker or colleague, identify ways in which your work at school, job or home can be redesigned to reduce stress and increase productivity. Use the hints provided in this book to guide your redesign.

5. Write a personal mission statement. Specify precisely your core principles; those things you consider to be central to your life and your sense of self-worth; and the legacy you want to leave. Identify at least one action you can take in order to accomplish that mission statement. Begin working on it today.

6. Establish a short-term goal or plan that you wish to accomplish this year. Make it compatible with the top priorities in your life. Specify the behavioural action steps, the reporting and accounting mechanisms, and the criteria of success and rewards as outlined in Figure 4 (page 00). Share this plan with others you know so that you have an incentive to pursue it even after you finish this assignment.

7. Get a physical examination, then outline and implement a regular physical fitness and diet programme. Even if it is just regular walking, do some kind of physical exercise at least three times a week. Preferably, institute a regular, vigorous cardiovascular fitness programme. Record your progress in your diary.
8. Pick at least one long-term deep-relaxation technique. Learn it and practice it on a regular basis. Record your progress in your diary.
9. Establish a mentoring relationship with someone with whom you work or go to college with. Your mentor may be a tutor, a senior manager or someone who has been around longer than you have. Make certain that the relationship is reciprocal and that it will help you cope with the stresses you face at work or college.

Application Plan and Evaluation

The intent of this exercise is to help you apply your time-management skills to real life. Unlike a 'training' activity, in which feedback is immediate and others can assist you with their evaluations, this skill application activity is one you must accomplish and evaluate on your own. There are two parts to this activity.

Part 1 helps prepare you to apply the skill. Part 2 helps you evaluate and improve on your experience. Be sure to write down answers to each item. Don't short-circuit the process by skipping steps.

Part 1 – Planning
1. Write down two or three aspects of this skill that are most important to you. These may be areas of weakness, areas you most want to improve or areas that are most salient to a problem you face right now. Identify the specific aspects of this skill that you want to apply.
2. Now identify the setting or the situation in which you will apply this skill. Establish a plan for performance by actually writing down a description of the situation. Who else will be involved? When will you do it? Where will it be done?
3. Identify the specific behaviours you will engage in to apply this skill. Operationalise your skill performance.
4. What are the indicators of successful performance? How will you know you have been effective? What will indicate you have performed competently?

Part 2 – Evaluation

5. After you have completed your implementation, record the results. What happened? How successful were you? What was the effect on others?

6. How can you improve? What modifications can you make next time? What will you do differently in a similar situation in the future?

7. Looking back on your whole skill practice and application experience, what have you learned? What has been surprising? In what ways might this experience help you in the long term?

Scoring Key

Stress Management

Skill area	Items	Assessment pre-	post-
Eliminating stressors	1, 5, 8, 9	——	——
Developing resilience	2, 3, 6, 7	——	——
Short-term coping	4, 10	——	——
Effective delegating	11, 12, 13, 14, 15	——	——
TOTAL SCORE		——	——

To assess how well you scored on this instrument, compare your scores to three comparison standards:
- The maximum score possible (90).
- The scores of other students in your class.
- Norm group consisting of 500 business school students.

In comparison to the norm group, if you scored:
70 or above, you are in the top quartile;
64 to 69, you are in the second quartile;
58 to 63, you are in the third quartile;
57 or below, you are in the bottom quartile.

Time Management

To determine how effective you are as a manager of your time, add together the frequency number you recorded for each activity.

Points	Frequency
0	Never
1	Seldom
2	Sometimes
3	Usually
4	Always

If you completed only Section 1 of the instrument, double the scores for each category.

If you scored 120 or above, you are an excellent manager of your time both personally and at work. If you scored between 100 and 120, you are doing a good job of managing your time and making a few refinements or implementing a few hints will help you achieve excellence. If you scored between 80 and 100, you should consider improving your time-management skills. If you scored below 80, training in time management will considerably enhance your efficiency.

Note: Sometimes people have markedly different scores in the two sections of this instrument. That is, they are better time managers at the office than in their personal lives, or vice versa. You may want to compute your scores for each section of the instrument and compare them.

Type A Personality Inventory

The Type A personality consists of four behavioural tendencies:
- Extreme competitiveness
- Significant life imbalance (typically coupled with high work involvement)
- Strong feelings of hostility and anger
- An extreme sense of urgency and impatience.

Scores above 12 in each area suggest this is a pronounced tendency.

Research suggests that the hostility aspect of the Type A personality is the most damaging to personal health.

Competitiveness			Life Imbalance (work involvement)	
Item	Score		Item	Score
1	____		2	____
5	____		6	____
9	____		10	____
13	____		14	____
17	____		18	____
21	____		22	____
Total	____		Total	____

Hostility/Anger			Impatience/Urgency	
Item	Score		Item	Score
3	____		4	____
7	____		8	____
11	____		12	____
15	____		16	____
19	____		20	____
23	____		24	____
Total	____		Total	____

TOTAL SCORE: _____

Glossary

Anticipatory stress	Stress arising from expected events.
Autonomy	The freedom to choose how and when to do a particular task.
Behaviour	Actions that can be seen, felt and measured in other people.
Brainstorming	A technique designed to help people solve problems by generating numerous alternative solutions without premature evaluation or rejection.
Cognitive style	The manner in which an individual gathers and evaluates the information that he or she receives. How we think.
Cognitive style strategies	Particular problem-solving patterns established by individuals in the way they take in, process and store information.
Deep relaxation	An approach for use in building psychological resilience in which both body and mind become completely relaxed.
Delegation	Allocation of responsibilities to another – usually in business, to a subordinate.
Enactive strategy	A method of managing stress that creates a new environment by eliminating the stressors.
Encounter stress	A type of stress that results from interpersonal conflict.
Environmental stress	A type of stress created by factors outside the control of the individual – forced change, reduced budgets, threats of redundancy.
Fixation	A defence mechanism against stress in which an individual simply continues with a response regardless of its merit e.g., repeatedly re-dialling the same telephone number.
Hardiness	A combination of the three characteristics of a highly stress-resistant personality – control, commitment and challenge.
Interpersonal competence	The ability to manage conflict, to build and manage teams, to coach and council, to provide valuable feedback, to influence and to be otherwise effective as a human being with other human beings.
Life balance	The development of resilience in all areas of one's life in order to handle unavoidable stress.
Management by Objectives (MBO)	A highly popular management technique of the 70's by which a subordinate's job is subdivided into distinct steps, each of which has a tight and measurable goal. These goals form the basis of an appraisal system.
Mentor	Usually, and in management where a more mature manager

	acts as an adviser, giving help to a new and inexperienced manager.
Pareto's law	A general 'wise saying' that 20 per cent of virtually any sample produces 80 per cent of the 'important' effect. For example, 20 per cent of customers generate 80 per cent of our profits.
Proactive strategy	A method of managing stress that initiates action in order to resist the negative aspects.
Problem solving	A jargon term for dealing with unusual and different management issues. It implies a process of analysis, collecting alternatives, collating the alternatives and judging the most likely to succeed.
Reactive strategy	A method of managing stress that copes with the immediate stressors, temporarily reducing their ill effects.
Regression	A strategy to reduce stress in which an individual adopts a behaviour pattern from the past, e.g., becomes childish.
Repression	A strategy to reduce stress in which an individual simply denies the stress exists.
Small-wins strategy	A strategy that individuals use to cope with stress involving a division of a large task into small elements, so that a mini victory celebration can be held at each small success.
Stereotype	An unevaluated view of another thing or person based on prejudice or previous experience.
Stressors	Stimuli that may cause physical and psychological reactions in individuals.
Time management	Strategy for reducing stress caused by issues of insufficient or excess time.
Type A personality	A hard driving, potentially hostile, intense and highly competitive personality.
Work redesign	A rethinking of the method of working to improve some measure – e.g., efficiency or sickness.

References

Adler, V. Little control equals lots of stress. *Psychology Today*, 1989, 23 (4), 18-19.

Anderson, C. R. Locus of control, coping behaviors and performance in a stress setting: A longitudinal study. *Journal of Applied Psychology*, 1977, 62, 446-451.

Antonovsky, A. *Health, stress and coping*. San Francisco: Jossey-Bass, 1979.

Beary, J. F. & Benson, H. A simple psychophysiologic technique which elicits the hypometabolic changes in the relaxation response. *Psychosomatic Medicine*, 1977, 36, 115-120.

Beehr, T. A. Perceived situational moderators of the relationship between subjective role ambiguity and role strain. *Journal of Applied Psychology*, 1976, 61, 35-40.

Benson, H. *The relaxation response*. New York: William Morrow, 1975.

Cameron, K. S. Strategies for successful organizational downsizing. *Human Resource Management Journal*, 1994, 33, 12-35.

Cameron, K. S. & Whetton, D. A. Organisational dysfunctions of decline. *Academy of Management Journal*, 1987, 30, 126-138.

Cameron, Kim S., Freeman, Sarah & Mishra, Aneil. Effective organizational downsizing: Paradoxical processes and best practices. *Academy of Management Executive*, 1990 (in press).

Carlson, S. *Executive behavior: A study of the work load and the working methods of managing directors*. Stockholm: Strombergs, 1951.

Cooper, M. J. & Aygen, M. M. A relaxation technique in the management of hypocholesterolemia. *Journal of Human Stress*, 1979, 5, 24-27.

Cooper, C. L. & Davidson, M. J. The high cost of stress on women managers. *Organizational Dynamics*, 1982, 11, 44-53.

Cooper, C. L., Cooper, R. D. & Eaker, L. H. *Living with stress*. London: Penguin Books, 1988.

Covey, Steven. *Seven habits of highly effective people*. New York: Wiley, 1988.

Covey, Steven. *Executive excellence*, December 1989, 6, 12, 7-8.

Curtis, John D. & Detert, Richard A. *How to relax: A holistic approach to stress management*. Palo Alto: Mayfield Publishing Co., 1981, 134.

Davidson, M. J. & Sutherland, V. J. Stress and construction site management – issues for Europe 1992. *Employee Relations*, 1992, 14, 2, 25-38.

Davis, M., Eshelman, E. & McKay, M., *The relaxation and stress reduction workbook*. Richmond, Calif.: New Harbinger Publications, 1980, 82.

Dyer, William G. *Teambuilding*. Reading, Mass.: Addison-Wesley, 1981.

Eliot, Robert S. & Breo, Dennis L. *Is it worth dying for?* New York: Bantam Books, 1984.

Farnham, A. Who beats stress best and how? *Fortune*, Oct 7, 1991, 71-86.

Freedman, J. L. & Fraser, S. C. Compliance without pressure: The foot-in-the-door technique. *Journal of Personality and Social Psychology*, 1966, 4, 195-202.

French, J. R. R. & Caplan, R. D. Organizational stress and individual strain. In A. J. Marrow (Ed.), *The failure of success*. New York: AMACOM, 1972.

Friedman, M. & Rosenman, R. H. Association of a specific overt behavior pattern with blood and cardiovascular findings. *Journal of the American Medical Association*, 1959, 169, 1286-1296.

Friedman, M. & Rosenman, R. H. *Type A behavior and your heart*. New York: Knopf, 1974.

Gill, L. Run ragged by the rat race. *The Times*, 5 January 1987.

Goldberg, H. *The hazards of being male*. New York: Nash, 1976.

Goldberg, H. *Executive health*. New York: McGraw-Hill, 1978.

Greenberg, J. *Comprehensive stress management* (2nd ed.). Dubuque, Ia.: Wm. C. Brown Publishers, 1987.

Griest, J. H. *et al*. Running as treatment for depression. *Comparative Psychiatry*, 1979, 20, 41-56.

Guest, R. H. Of time and the foreman. *Personnel*, 1956, 32, 478-486.

Hackman, J. R. & Oldham, G. R. Development of the job diagnostic survey. *Journal of Applied Psychology*, 1975, 60, 159-170.

Hackman, J. R., Oldham, G. R., Janson, R. & Purdy, K. A new strategy for job enrichment. *California Management Review*, 1975, 17, 57-71.

Hall, D. T. *Careers in organizations*. Santa Monica, Calif.: Goodyear, 1976.

Hamner, W. C. & Organ, D. W. *Organizational behavior: An applied psychological approach*. Dallas: Business Publications, 1978.

Hingley, P. & Cooper, C. L. *Stress and the nurse manager*. London: 1986.

Hollander, S. *The sources of increased efficiency*. Cambridge, Mass.: MIT Press, 1965.

Holmes, T. H. & Masuda, M. Life change and illness susceptibility. In B. S. Dohnrenwend & B. P. Dohrenwend (Eds.) *Stressful life events: Their nature and effects*. New York: Wiley, 1974.

Holmes, T. H. & Rahe, R. H. The social reajustment rating scale. *Journal of Psychosomatic Research*. 1967, 11, 213-218.

Holmes, T. H. & Rahe, R. H. The social reajustment rating scale. *Journal of Psychosomatic Research*, 1970, 14, 121-132.

Holmes, T. S. & Holmes T. H. Short-term intrusions into the lifestyle routine. *Journal of Psychosomatic Research*, 1970, 14, 121–32.

Ivancevich, John M. & Matteson, Michael T. *Stress & work: A managerial perspective.* Glenview, Ill.: Scott Foresman, 1980.

Jenkins, C. D. Recent evidence supporting psychological and social risk factors in coronary disease. *New England Journal of Medicine*, 1976, 294, 1033–1034.

Jourard, S. M. *The transparent self.* Princeton, N.J.: Von Nostrand, 1964.

Kamiya, J. Conscious control of brain power. *Psychology Today*, 1978, 1, 57–60.

Kearns, J. *Stress at work: The challenge of change.* BUPA, 1986.

Kobasa, Salvadore. Commitment and coping in stress resistance among lawyers. *Journal of Personality and Social Psychology*, 1982, 42, 707–717.

Kobasa, S. C. Stressful life events, personality, and health: An inquiry into hardiness. *Journal of Personality and Social Psychology*, 1979, 37, 1–12.

Kotter, John. *The general managers.* New York: Free Press, 1987.

Kram, Kathy. *Mentoring at work.* Glenview, Ill.: Scott Foresman, 1985.

Kuhn, A. & Beam, R. D. *The logic of organizations.* San Francisco: Jossey-Bass, 1982.

Levinson, J. D. *Seasons of a man's life.* New York: Knopf, 1978.

Lewin, K. *Field theory in social science.* New York: Harper & Row, 1951.

Likert, Rensis. *The human organization.* New York: McGraw-Hill, 1967.

Luthe, Wolfgang. Method, research and application of autogenic training. *American Journal of Clinical Hypnosis*, 1962, 5, 17–23.

Maddi, Salvadore & Kobasa, Suzanne C. *The hardy executive: Health under stress.* Homewood, Ill.: Dow Jones-Irwin, 1984.

Mednick, M. T. Woman and the psychology of achievement: Implications for personal and social change. In H. J. Bernardin (Ed.), *Women in the workforce.* New York: Praeger, 1982.

Milgram, Stanley. Behavioral study of obedience. *Journal of Abnormal and Social Psychology*, 1963, 63, 371–378.

Mintzberg, Henry. *The nature of managerial work.* New York: Harper & Row, 1973.

Mishra, A. K. *Organizational response to crisis.* Unpublished doctoral dissertation, University of Michigan, 1993.

Orme-Johnson, D. W. Autonomic stability and transcendental meditation. *Psychosomatic Medicine*, 1973, 35, 341–349.

Perl, Lila. *Junk food, fast food, health food.* New York: Clarion Books, 1980.

Rahe, R. H. The pathway between subjects' recent life change and their near future illness reports: Representative results and methodological issues. In B. S. Dohrenwend & B. P. Dohrenwend (Eds.). *Stressful life events: Their nature and effects.* New York: Wiley, 1974.

Rahe, R. H., Ryman, D. H. & Ward, H. W. Simplified scaling for life change events. *Journal of Human Stress*, 1980, 6, 22-27.

Sayles, Leonard. *Managerial behavior: Administration in complex organizations.* New York: McGraw-Hill, 1964.

Schein, Edgar H. Interpersonal communication, group solidarity, and social influence. *Sociometry*, 1960, 23, 148-161.

Schachter, S. *The psychology of affiliation: Experimental studies of the sources of gregariousness.* Stanford, Calif.: Stanford University Press, 1959.

Sculley, John. *Odyssey: Pepsi to Apple.* London: Fontana, 1989.

Shaw, M.E. *Group dynamics: The psychology of small group behavior.* (2nd ed.). New York: McGraw-Hill, 1976.

Staw, Barry M., Sandelands, Lance & Dutton, Jane. Threat-rigidity effects in organizational behavior. *Administrative Science Quarterly*, 1981, 26, 501-524.

Stone, R. A. & Deleo, J. Psychotherapeutic control of hypertension. *New England Journal of Medicine*, 1976, 294, 80-84.

Summers, D. Testing for stress in the workplace. *Financial Times*, 6 December 1990.

Weick, Karl. *The social psychology of organizing.* Reading, Mass.: Addison-Wesley, 1979.

Weick, Karl. Small wins. *American Psychologist*, 1984, 39, 40-49.

Weick, K. *The KOR experiment.* Working paper, University of Michigan Graduate School of Business, 1993.

Wolff, H. G., Wolf, S. G. & Hare, C. C. (Eds.). *Life stress and bodily disease.* Baltimore: Williams and Wilkins, 1950.

Wolman, Benjamin B. (Ed.). *Psychological aspects of obesity: A handbook.* New York: Von Nostrand Reinhold, 1982.

Woods, Mike & Whitehead, Jackie. *Working Alone.* London: Pitman, 1993.

Index

stress management
   behavioural guidelines exercises, 70
stress reduction techniques – temporary
   deep breathing, 68
   imagery and fantasy, 68
   muscle relaxation, 68
   reframing, 69
   rehearsal, 69
stressors, 13
   anticipatory, 23
   elimination of , 24, 37, 41, 44
   encounter, 21
   situational, 22
   time stressors, 20
Summers, D., 11
supportive social relations, 65

time management
   basic rules, 31
   dimensions of priority, 34
   effective, 25
   elimination of stressors by, 24
time management matrix, 26
time management survey, 31
   rules of, 31

transcendental meditation, 64
type A personality, 58
   characteristics of, 58
   heart disease, 59
   inventory, 6
   percentages in USA, 59
   sex linked behaviour, 60
   smoking habits, 59
type B personality, 59

Unilever, 68

Vietnam, 65
Volvo, 44

Weick, K. E., 13, 18, 24, 49, 63
Western hostages in Iran and Beirut, 23
Wolf, Dr Stewart, 38
Wolff, H. G., Wolf, S. G. & Hare, C. C., 22
Wolman, B. B., 54
Woods, M. & Whitehead, J., 38
work design to eliminate stressors, 41

Zen Buddhism, 60